Cute Cats & Teddy Bears

Cute Cats
&
Teddy Bears

25 Delightful Cross-stitch Pictures to Sew

Debbie Minton

COLLINS & BROWN

Distributed by
Trafalgar Square
North Pomfret, Vermont 05053

To my husband and best friend, Graham, for putting up with me while I was writing this book and to my late father for introducing me to the wonderful world of needlework when I was a little girl.

First published in Great Britain in 1998
by Collins & Brown Ltd
London House
Great Eastern Wharf
Parkgate Road
London SW11 4NQ

1 3 5 7 9 8 6 4 2

British Library Cataloguing-in-Publication Data:
A catalogue record for this book
is available from the British Library.

ISBN 1 85585 492 9 (hardback edition)
ISBN 1 85585 601 8 (paperback edition)

Designer: Sara Kidd
Photographer: Shona Wood

Reproduction by Hong Kong Graphic and Printing Ltd
Printed and bound in Spain by Graficas Estella

Contents

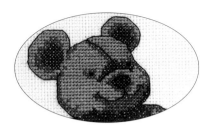

Introduction

CATS AND TEDDY BEARS have always been a passion of mine.

I have various collections of ornamental cats from china, to resin to crystal. I am always on the lookout for cat pictures, greeting cards and so on to give me ideas for my designs but the best way I have found is from watching the real thing! I have two cats who are full of fun and character and who always greet me when I come home from work with miaows ranging from 'where have you been' to 'where's my tea, I'm hungry'!

Cats have such appealing faces and you will find that you will probably be spoilt for choice as to which cat design to stitch first.

As for bears, well I have had a passion for bears for as long as I can remember. I have a collection of soft bears on my bed, silver bears on my window ledges, crystal bears in my lounge, and stone bears in my garden. Every one of my bears has a name and to me they are all real.

To design and stitch my favourite creatures is paradise to me. My father taught me how to stitch from a very early age. He showed me a table cloth where his mother had stitched one corner and my father stitched another corner. When I was about 17 years old my father gave me the table cloth and asked me to stitch the third corner and when my daughter was born, 20 years ago, he asked me if I would ask her to stitch the final corner. A real family heirloom.

I tell people that you can get easily get hooked on cross stitch and it's true. Both my sons stitch and my daughter just about managed to put her stitching down to study for her exams. I have been found many a night, fast asleep with my needle and project on my lap having literally stitched myself to sleep.

Here I have given you some different ideas on how to adapt these pictures and using waste canvas, you can stitch any of the pictures onto an item of clothing or even a pillowslip or duvet cover.

I'm sure you will spend many happy hours stitching the designs and looking at the finished pictures in your home. I hope they give you as much pleasure as they do me. Have fun!

Debbie Minton

Fun in the Garden

These two cheeky cats are up to mischief as they play amongst the flower pots. One cat has knocked over two flower pots while the other cat is chasing a spider. My two cats always join me when I am gardening and they, too, are always up to no good.

ACTUAL DESIGN SIZE:
5¾ x 11½ in (14.5 x 29 cm)

MATERIALS
✦ 1 piece of 14-count Zweigart Aida in white measuring approximately 10¾ x 16½ in (27 x 42 cm)
✦ No. 24 tapestry needle

This cat sits innocently amongst the flower pots it has knocked over.

INSTRUCTIONS
Mark the centre of the chart. Find the centre of your material and make long tacking stitches across and down as your guides. Using two strands of stranded cotton unless otherwise stated (except for backstitching where you use one strand unless otherwise stated) begin your work following the chart. For full instructions on how to make half-cross stitches, cross stitches, backstitches, special shaping stitches, long stitches and French knots, see *Techniques* section on pages 125–127 of this book.

THREADS

DMC Colours	Metres
White	3
310 black	2
413 light charcoal grey	4
317 dark grey	2
318 medium grey	3
762 very pale grey	1
353 light salmon pink	2
747 pale blue	1
3820 mustard	2
606 red	3

300 very dark brown	3
301 dark ginger	2
3345 light bottle green	2
580 dark green	2
3347 sage green	6
3819 lime green	3
720 tan	4
722 dull orange	2
972 bright yellow	1
970 orange	1
3799 charcoal grey	1
817 dark red	2
935 bottle green	2

COLOURS FOR BACKSTITCHING

Backstitch watering can using 3345 (two strands).

Backstitch watering can rose and vertical lines in rose using 301.

Backstitch pouncing cat using 3799.

Backstitch flowers using 817.

Rest of backstitching use 310.

LONG STITCHES

Cats whiskers use white.

Hairs in cats' ears use 413.

Spider's legs and bee's legs and antennae use 310.

Stalks on flowers use 935 (3 strands).

FRENCH KNOTS

Whisker dots on cats use 413.

Cats' eyes use white.

Watering can handle use 3345.

HALF-CROSS STITCHES

For grass use 3345 (one strand).

KEY

White – Markings on cats	353 Ears, nose, mouth of cats
310 Bee, eyes, spider	747 Bee's wings
413 Seated cat	3820 Watering can rose
317 Shading on pouncing cat	606 Flower petals
318 Pouncing cat	300 Edge of soil
762 Face and paws on pouncing cat	301 Soil

 3345 In watering can, bolts, stripe

580 Shading on leaves

3347 Watering can

3819 Leaves

720 Plant pots

722 Plant pot highlights

972 Centres of flowers and bees

970 Shading on petals

Moonlight Serenade

....

Here are three cats singing harmoniously under the stars — although I'm sure their neighbours would disagree! I have used navy Aida as it really does give the feeling of a night-time scene. A useful tip when using navy is to put a white pillowslip or tea towel on your knee as you will then be able to see the holes much more easily.

ACTUAL DESIGN SIZE:
9 x 11 in (23 x 28 cm)

MATERIALS
✦ 1 piece of 14-count Zweigart Aida in navy blue measuring approximately 13¾ x 15¾ in (35 x 40 cm)
✦ No. 24 tapestry needle

INSTRUCTIONS
Mark the centre of the chart. Find the centre of your material and make long tacking stitches across and down. Using two strands of stranded cotton (except for backstitching where you use one strand only unless otherwise stated) begin your work following the chart. Full instructions for cross stitches, backstitches, special shaping stitches, long stitches and French knots are in the *Techniques* section on pages 125–127.

THREADS

DMC Colour	Metres
310 black	5
317 dark grey	9
762 very pale grey	5
839 dark mink brown	4
841 light mink brown	6
918 dark cinnamon	3
920 cinnamon	4
922 pale cinnamon	2
581 light sage green	1
745 pale yellow	3
817 dark red	8
350 dark coral	9
352 salmon pink	4
353 light salmon pink	1
754 peach	1
3371 very dark brown	2
3799 charcoal grey	2
743 bright yellow	1

COLOURS FOR BACKSTITCHING
Backstitch on brown cat using 3371.
Backstitch eyes, noses and mouths on grey cats using 310.
Rest of backstitching on grey cats use 3799.
Backstitch on roof and chimney using 310 (two strands).
Backstitch around moon using 743.

LONG STITCHES
Cats whiskers use 762.
Stars use 743.

FRENCH KNOTS
Whisker dots on grey cats use 317.
Eyes on grey cats use 762.
Whisker dots on brown cat use 3371.

*A moonlit night is perfect for these feline friends
to sing romantic ballads to each other.*

KEY

310	Pupils of grey cats' eyes
317	Grey cats
762	Grey cats' paws, tail tips, fronts
839	Shading on brown cat
841	Brown cat
918	Dark marks on chimney
920	Light marks on chimney
922	Chimney
581	Grey cats' eyes
745	Moon
817	Dark shading on roof
350	Roof
352	Light shading on roof
353	Brown cat's nose and inside ears
754	Grey cats' noses and inside ears

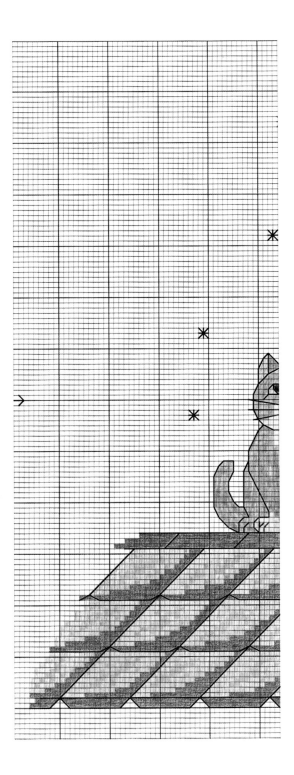

Sweet Dreams

Have you noticed how content cats look when they are sleeping? This cat is no exception. It looks warm and cosy, fast asleep on its pillow. The surrounding patchwork makes a colourful frame and you can change the colours of the patchwork to match your own colour schemes.

ACTUAL DESIGN SIZE:
8 x 10 in (20 x 25.5 cm)

MATERIALS
◆ 1 piece of 14-count Zweigart Aida in white measuring approximately 13 x 15 in (33 x 38 cm)
◆ No. 24 tapestry needle

INSTRUCTIONS
Mark the centre of the chart. Make long tacking stitches across and down the centre of your material. Using two strands of stranded cotton (except for backstitching where you use one strand unless otherwise stated) begin your work following the chart. For full instructions for cross stitches, backstitches, special shaping stitches, long stitches and French knots, see the *Techniques* section on pages 125–127.

THREADS

DMC Colour	Metres
743 bright yellow	7
745 pale yellow	10
741 light orange	3
746 cream	7
340 lilac	4
3747 pale lilac	8
3746 dark lilac	2
792 blue	8
747 pale blue	10
964 light mint green	8
943 jade green	3
3023 stone	5
3787 dark stone	5
963 pink	7
3824 pale peach	1
333 purple	2
3021 brown	2
3371 very dark brown	1
451 grey	2
701 green	2
602 deep pink	3
995 electric blue	2

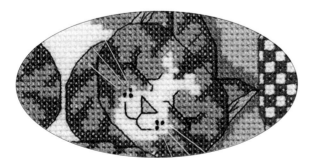

You can tell from this cat's face that it is deep in the middle of a happy dream.

COLOURS FOR BACKSTITCHING

Backstitch on and around pillow using 333.

Backstitch cat using 3021.

Backstitch cat's eyes, nose and mouth using 3371.

Backstitch around individual patchwork hexagons using 451.

Backstitch orange spots using 741.

Backstitch blue squares on gingham hexagon using 792.

Backstitch leaves on flowered hexagon using 701 (two strands).

LONG STITCHES

Cat's whiskers use 746 (one strand).

Pale yellow hexagons use 602.

Hairs in cat's ears use 3021.

FRENCH KNOTS

Whisker dots on cat use 3371.

French knots on flowered hexagon use 995.

Key

	743 Large spotty hexagon
	745 Diamond hexagon
	741 Large spots
	746 Cat shading, gingham
	340 Shading on pillow
	3747 Pillow
	3746 Small dots
	792 Dark gingham colour
	747 Flower hexagon
	964 Striped hexagon
	943 Stripes
	3023 Cat
	3787 Dark colour on cat
	963 Small dotted hexagon
	3824 Cat's ears and nose

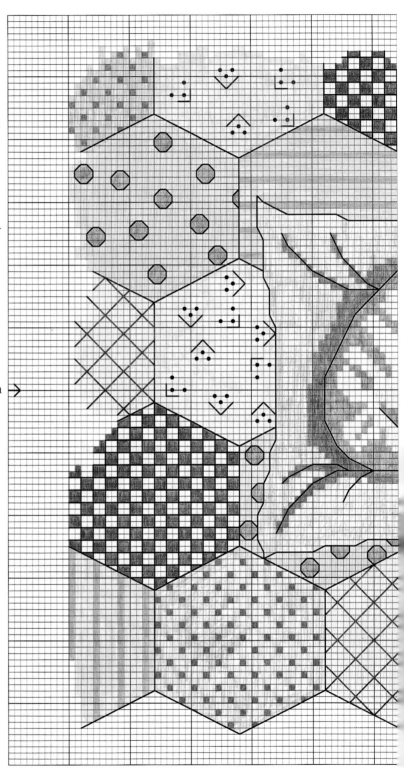

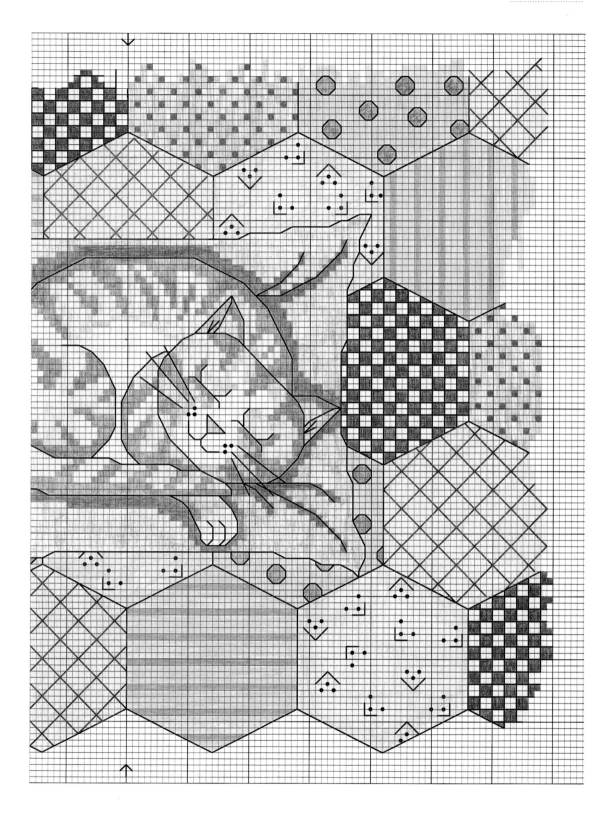

Hide and Seek

When my cats were tiny kittens, one of their favourite games was to hide amongst the clean washing that was still warm from the tumble dryer. This picture is typical of the fun and warmth that cats crave and it is the type of design that you could put in the kitchen or even the bathroom.

ACTUAL DESIGN SIZE:
6½ x 13 in (16.5 x 33 cm)

MATERIALS
◆ 1 piece of 14-count Zweigart Aida in white measuring approximately 11½ x 18 in (29 x 46 cm)
◆ No. 24 tapestry needle

INSTRUCTIONS
Mark the centre of the chart. Find the centre of your material and make long tacking stitches across and down. Using two strands of stranded cotton (except for backstitching where you use one strand unless otherwise stated) begin your work following the chart. For full instructions for cross stitches, backstitches, special shaping stitches, long stitches and French knots, see the *Techniques* section on pages 125–127.

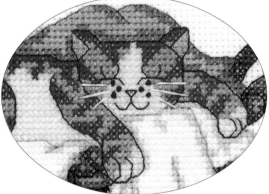

This little cat has grown tired of playing and has fallen asleep in the washing basket.

THREADS

DMC Colour	Metres
310 black	1
829 dark golden brown	1
801 dark brown	4
434 brown	3
435 light brown	7
437 beige	3
976 ginger	1
720 tan	2
676 pale mustard	1
349 dull red	10
3325 blue	3
775 pale blue	5
341 lilac	1
3747 pale lilac	1
913 apple green	1
955 light apple green	1
581 light sage green	1
744 yellow	2
745 pale yellow	2

746 cream	7
722 pale orange	3
3824 pale peach	1
762 pale grey	3
3756 hint of blue	1
white	4
919 brick	1
322 mid blue	3
415 grey	1
340 dark lilac	1
743 bright yellow	1

COLOURS FOR BACKSTITCHING

Backstitch ginger cats using 919.
Backstitch tabby cat using 829.
Backstitch laundry basket using 801.
Backstitch around blue checked washing using 322 (two strands).
Backstitch green washing using 913.
Backstitch white washing using 415.
Backstitch lilac washing using 340.
Backstitch yellow washing using 743.

Backstitch sock using 322.
Backstitch red floor tiles using 349.
(two strands)

LONG STITCHES

Blue checked washing use 322 (one strand).
Cats' whiskers use white.

FRENCH KNOTS

Whisker dots on ginger cats use 919.
Whisker dots on tabby cat use 829.

KEY

- 310 Cats' pupils
- 829 Tabby's face, paw, dark
- 801 Shading on basket
- 434 Sticks on basket
- 435 Dark basket weave
- 437 Light basket weave
- 976 Tabby cat's face, paw
- 720 Ginger cats' stripes
- 676 Tabby's face, paw, light
- 349 Floor tiles
- 3325 Sock, check washing
- 775 Checked washing
- 341 Shading, lilac washing
- 3747 Lilac washing
- 913 Shading, green washing
- 955 Green washing
- 581 Cats' eyes
- 744 Shading, yellow washing
- 745 Yellow washing
- 746 Ginger cats, floor tiles
- 722 Ginger cats
- 3824 Cats' noses, inside ears
- 762 Shading, white washing
- 3756 Trim on sock
- White – White washing

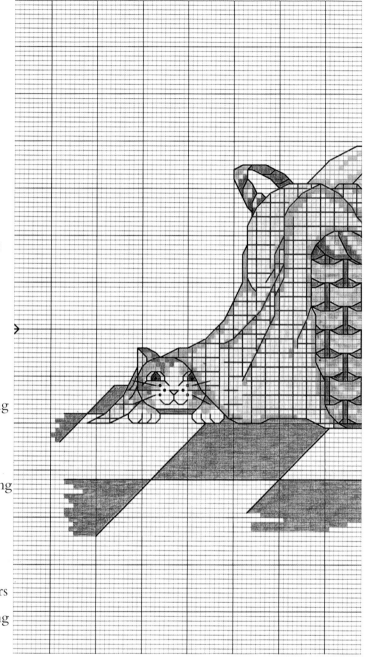

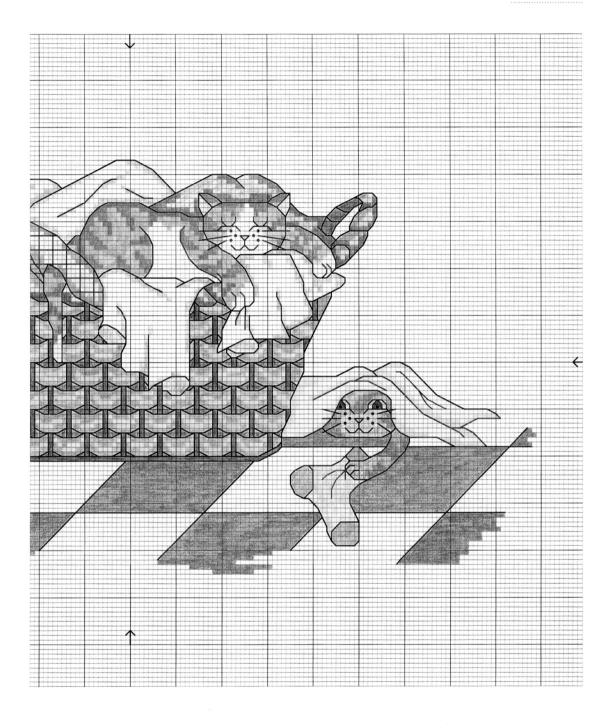

Tin Can Alley

Here are cats making mischief. They have knocked over the dustbin and have scattered scraps of food everywhere. If your cats are anything like mine, they will still try to get food from the dustbin even though they are well-fed, fat cats! This picture makes a perfect partner to the Alley Cats on page 36.

ACTUAL DESIGN SIZE:
6¾ x 11¾ in (17 x 30 cm)

MATERIALS
◆ 1 piece of 32-count Belfast Linen in white – 16-count white Aida can be used instead measuring approximately

11¾ x 16½ in (30 x 42 cm)
◆ No. 24 tapestry needle

INSTRUCTIONS
Mark the centre of the chart. Find the centre of your material and make long tacking stitches across and down. Using

two strands of stranded cotton (except for backstitching where you use one strand unless stated otherwise) begin your work following the chart. For instructions on cross stitches, backstitches, special shaping stitches, half-cross stitches and French knots, see the *Techniques* section on pages 125–127.

THREADS

DMC Colour	Metres
318 medium grey	6
415 light grey	7
762 very pale grey	5
414 grey	1
317 dark grey	1
646 dark stone	1
3072 stone	1
726 lemon	1
676 pale mustard	1
740 orange	1
720 tan	2
721 dull orange	3
742 deep yellow	1
3824 pale peach	1
613 beige	2
611 dark beige	2
3781 brown	2
400 chestnut brown	1
3750 blue	1
931 blue/grey	1
356 terracotta	4
758 pale terracotta	4
704 pale green	1
701 green	1
White	3
310 black	2
3821 mustard	1

These cats are burrowing inside the bin in search of tasty pieces of food.

COLOURS FOR BACKSTITCHING
Fishbone use 3821 (two strands).
Apple and banana stalks use 400 (two strands).
Rest of backstitching use 310.

HALF-CROSS STITCHES
Shading on floor use 611.

FRENCH KNOTS
Cats' eye use white.
Whisker dots and all other French knots use 310.

KEY

- 318 Dark bin lines
- 415 Bin, tin can
- 762 Bin highlights
- 414 In bin, handles
- 317 Handles
- 646 Peeping cat
- 3072 Cat's nose
- 726 Banana skin
- 676 Apple core
- 740 Baked beans
- 720 Stripes, cat in bin
- 721 Cat in bin
- 742 Eyes, tin label
- 3824 Noses and ears
- 613 Cat on bin
- 611 Cat on bin
- 3781 Cat on bin
- 400 Banana, apple
- 3750 Fish – dark
- 931 Fish – light
- 356 Brickwork
- 758 Brickwork
- 704 Apple skin
- 701 Beans tin
- White – Litter
- 310 Cats' eyes

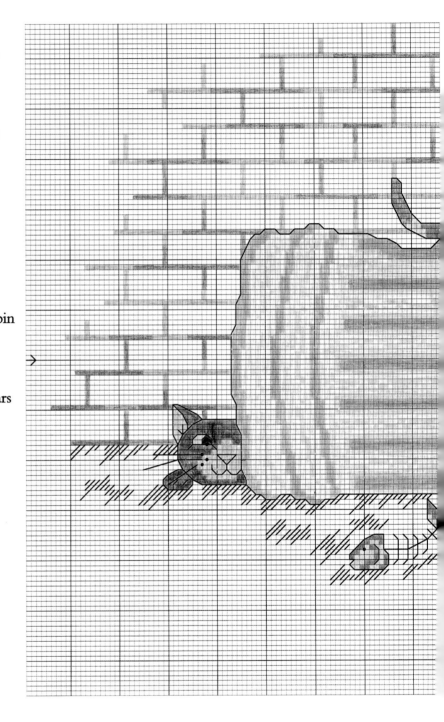

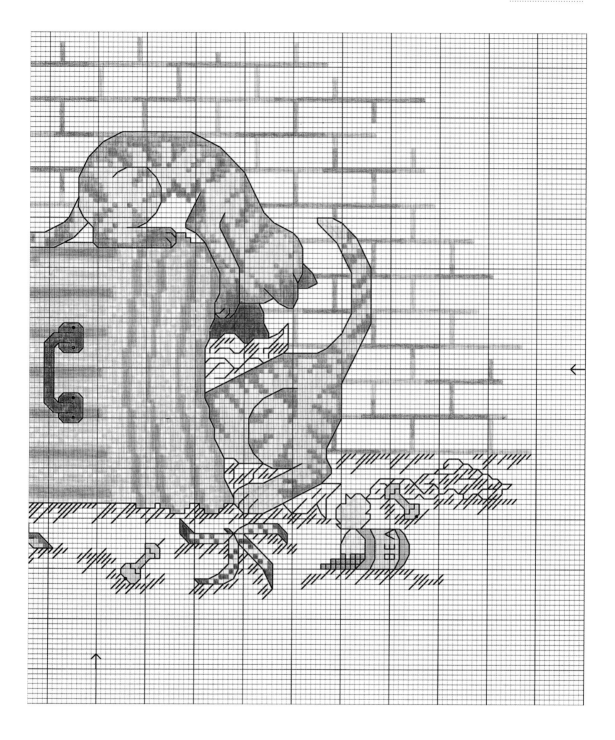

Balancing Act

If you have ever watched cats climbing you must have also watched them walking on the narrowest fences and walls. I am always fascinated by their amazing balancing acts and have put these two cute little cats on a wall for you to stitch. I have mounted this picture in a flexi-hoop but you could stitch it onto a towel, pillowslip or anything you like using waste canvas (see Techniques *section for instructions).*

ACTUAL DESIGN SIZE
3¾ x 2¾ in (9.5 x 7 cm)

MATERIALS
✦ 1 piece of 18-count Zweigart Aida in cream measuring approximately 8¾ x 7¾ in (22 x 19.5 cm)
✦ No. 24 tapestry needle
✦ Flexi-hoop (optional)

INSTRUCTIONS
Mark the centre of the chart. Find the centre of your material and make long tacking stitches across and down to use as your guides. Using two strands of stranded cotton (except for backstitching where you use one strand only unless otherwise stated) begin your work following the chart. For full instructions for cross stitches, backstitches, special shaping stitches, long stitches and French knots, see the *Techniques* section of this book on pages 125–127.

THREADS

DMC Colour	Metres
721 dull orange	2
722 pale orange	2
413 dark grey	2
3823 very pale yellow	1
469 olive green	1
704 light green	1
353 light salmon pink	1
758 light terracotta	2
3830 terracotta	3
310 black	1
white	1

COLOURS FOR BACKSTITCHING
All backstitching use 310.

LONG STITCHES
Cat's whiskers use white.
Hairs inside ginger cat's ears use 310.

FRENCH KNOTS
Whisker dots on cats use 310.

This cat sits on a wall, gossiping happily with its friend and watching the world go by.

KEY

	721 Stripes on big cat
	722 Big cat
	413 Little cat
	3823 Highlights on little cat
	469 Little cat's eyes
	704 Big cat's eyes
	353 Ears and noses
	758 Markings on wall
	3830 Wall

Dinner Time

When I am preparing dinner, my cats sit next to me in the kitchen looking up in anticipation of a tasty treat. I always picture them sitting at a table with a plate of fish in front of them. This is why this design is so appealing to me. You could stitch this design onto a tea towel, using waste canvas (see Techniques *section for instructions). I have stitched this design using one strand of stranded cotton, but if you wish to use two strands remember to double up on the thread quantities given below.*

ACTUAL DESIGN SIZE:
9½ x 8½ in (24 x 21.5 cm)

MATERIALS
◆ 1 piece of 18-count Zweigart Aida in cream measuring approximately 14½ x 13½ in (37 x 34 cm)
◆ No. 24 tapestry needle

INSTRUCTIONS
Mark the centre of the chart. Find the centre of your material and make long tacking stitches across and down. Using one strand only of stranded cotton for all cross stitches and backstitching unless otherwise stated begin your work following the chart. Full instructions for cross stitches, backstitches, special shaping stitches and long stitches see the *Techniques* section on pages 125–127.

THREADS

DMC Colour	Metres
301 dark ginger	1
310 black	1
353 light salmon pink	1
402 light ginger	2
413 dark grey	2
414 mid grey	1
415 grey	1
434 dark brown	2
435 brown	5
437 light brown	2
472 very light green	1
666 bright red	2
701 dark green	2
703 green	2
704 light green	2
725 dark yellow	1
726 yellow	1
727 pale yellow	1
762 very pale grey	1
930 dark blue grey	1
931 blue grey	1
932 light blue grey	1
995 electric blue	1
3776 ginger	1
white	3
352 salmon pink	1

COLOURS FOR BACKSTITCHING

Leaves on lettuce use 701.

Cats' mouths use 352.

Cats' eyes use 310.

Knot on napkin use white.

COLOURS FOR LONG STITCH

Cats whiskers and hair in ears use 2 strands of 762.

Stems of flowers on wallpaper use 701.

These cats have had a busy day playing and richly deserve their dinner.

KEY

	301
	310
	353
	402
	413
	414
	415
	434
	435
	437
	472
	666
	701
	703
	704
	725
	726
	727
	762
	930
	931
	932
	995
	3776
	White

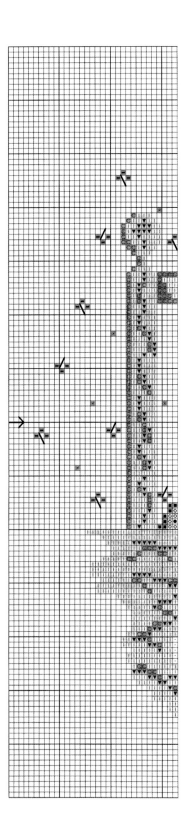

Alley Cats

Cats love going into dustbins for scraps of food and these two have been caught in the act. One cat has finished its meal but the other is still searching for food in the dustbin. This is a lovely picture to stitch; fun and full of character. I have stitched this design using one strand of stranded cotton, but if you wish to use two strands, remember to double up on the thread quantities given below.

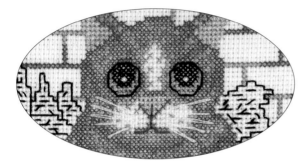

This little cat isn't as quick as its friend and is still searching for its supper.

ACTUAL DESIGN SIZE:
10½ x 7½ in (27 x 18.5 cm)

MATERIALS
✦ 1 piece of 18-count Zweigart Aida in cream measuring approximately 15½ x 12½ in (39 x 32 cm)
✦ No. 24 tapestry needle

INSTRUCTIONS
Mark the centre of the chart. Find the centre of your material and make long tacking stitches across and down. Using one strand only of stranded cotton for both cross stitches and backstitching begin your work following the chart. For full instructions for cross stitches, backstitches, special shaping stitches, half-cross stitches and long stitches, see the *Techniques* section on pages 125–127.

THREADS

DMC Colour	Metres
310 black	3
318 medium grey	3
353 light salmon pink	1
356 dusky pink	3
400 dark tan	1
415 light grey	4
469 olive green	1
611 dark beige	2
613 beige	2
704 light green	1
712 cream	3
720 tan	2
721 dull orange	2
722 pale orange	2
725 dark yellow	1
726 yellow	1
739 light beige	2
758 light terracotta	2
762 very pale grey	3
931 blue/grey	1

950 peach	1
3750 blue	1
3781 brown	2
white	3

KEY

▦	310
▦	318
▩	353
▦	356
▦	400
▦	415
▦	469
▦	611
▦	613
▦	704
▦	712
▦	720
▦	721
▦	722
▦	725
▦	726
▦	739
▦	758
▦	762
▦	931
▦	950
▦	3750
▦	3781
▦	White

COLOURS USED FOR BACKSTITCHING

Backstitch newspaper and bin handle using 310.
Backstitch tabby cat's mouth using 758.
Backstitch ginger cat's mouths using 356.
Backstitch tabby cat's tummy using 611.
Backstitch both cats' eyes using 310.

HALF-CROSS STITCHES

Shading on the floor use 611.

LONG STITCHES

Cats' whiskers and hair inside tabby cat's ears use 712.
Fish bones use 726.

Cat Nap

The tassels on the corner of the cushion make a perfect finishing touch to this sweet
design. The cat is so comfortable that it does not even wake up when the two mice
appear! I have mounted this in a gift card with the tassels just coming over the edge.
You could also frame it or stitch it onto an item of clothing or tea towel using waste
canvas (see Techniques *section for instructions*).

ACTUAL DESIGN SIZE;
2½ x 4 in (6 x 10 cm) including tassels

MATERIALS
◆ 1 piece of 18-count Zweigart Aida in white measuring approximately 7½ x 9 in (19 x 23 cm)
◆ No. 24 tapestry needle
◆ Gift card and envelope (optional)

INSTRUCTIONS
Mark the centre of the chart. Find the centre of your material and make long tacking stitches across and down. Using two strands of stranded cotton (except for backstitching where you use one strand only) begin your work following the chart. For full instructions for cross stitches, backstitches, special shaping stitches, long stitches and French knots, see *Techniques* section on pages 125–127.

THREADS

DMC Colour	Metres
3801 deep coral	4
761 pink	1
722 dull orange	2
972 bright yellow	1
413 dark grey	2
3827 light ginger	2
3823 very pale yellow	2
310 black	1

TASSELS
Before you do your backstitching, thread your needle with two strands of 972. Make approximately 10 loops in the front corners of the cushion, about half an inch long (12 mm) and secure at the back. Carefully trim the ends away to leave the tassels on your work. Refer to the finished picture for the positioning of tassels.

COLOURS FOR BACKSTITCHING
Use 310 for all backstitching.

LONG STITCHES
For cat's whiskers use 3823.

FRENCH KNOTS
For whisker dots on cat and eyes on mice use 310.

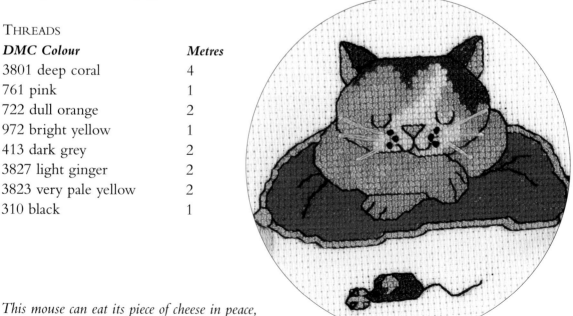

This mouse can eat its piece of cheese in peace, safe in the knowledge that the cat is fast asleep.

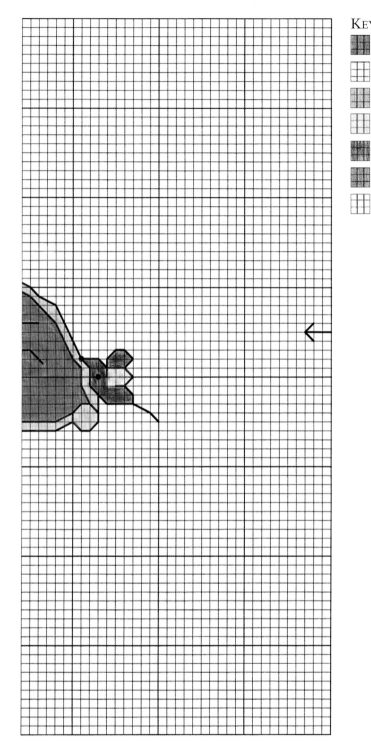

KEY

3801 Cushion

761 Inside cat's ears and nose

722 Cat and cheese

972 Cushion and cheese

413 Top of cat and mice

3827 Dark shading on cat

3823 Light shading on cat

Cat Among Flowers

··

I love this cute design of a cat peeping through flowers at a bee. I have set this in a silver-plated trinket box as the colour of the cat suits silver very well. You could also mount it in a gift card or simply put it in a frame (see Techniques section).

ACTUAL DESIGN SIZE:
2½ x 2¾ in (6 x 7 cm)

MATERIALS
✦ 1 piece of 16-count Zweigart Aida measuring approximately 7½ x 7¾ in (19 x 19.5 cm)
✦ No. 24 tapestry needle
✦ Silver-plated trinket box (optional)

INSTRUCTIONS
Mark the centre of the chart. Find the centre of your material and make long tacking stitches across and down. Using two strands of stranded cotton (except for backstitching where you use one strand only) begin your work following the chart. Full instructions for cross stitches, backstitches, special shaping stitches, long stitches and French knots are in the *Techniques* section on pages 125–127. Make up the trinket box following the manufacturer's instructions.

THREADS

DMC Colour	Metres
White	2
470 green	2
535 dark grey	2
3824 pale peach	1
963 pink	2
899 dark pink	2
309 light coral pink	2
3820 mustard	1
747 pale blue	1
326 dark coral pink	1
936 sage green	1
310 black	1

COLOURS FOR BACKSTITCHING
Backstitch flowers using 326.
Backstitch leaves using 936.
Backstitch cat and bee using 310.

LONG STITCHES
Cat's whiskers use white.
Refer to finished picture for positioning.

FRENCH KNOTS
Cat's eyes use white.
Whisker dots use 310.

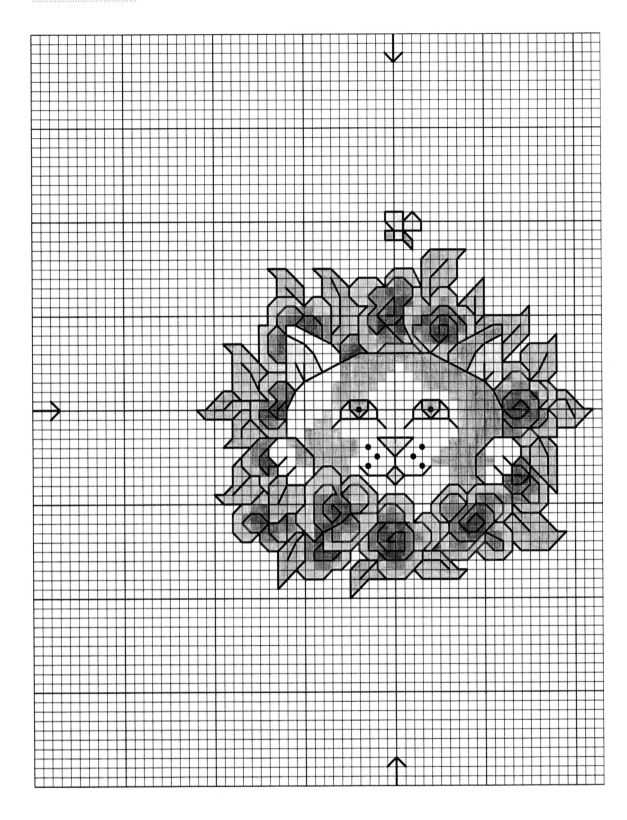

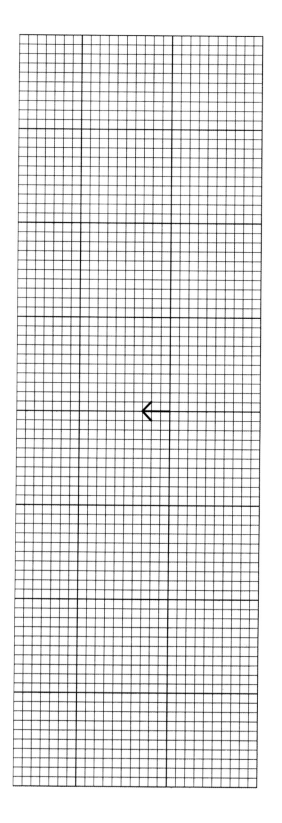

KEY

	White – Face, outer ears, paws
	470 Leaves
	535 Cat and bee
	3824 Inner ears, nose and mouth
	963 Light flower petals
	899 Medium flower petals
	309 Dark flower petals
	3820 Cat's eyes
	747 Bee's wings

This cat bashfully watches a busy bumble bee, tucked away in its bed of flowers.

A Misadventure

My cats hate water, but if they see a bird drinking from a puddle or the bird table, they somehow forget this dislike and approach them very eagerly! This poor ginger cat didn't jump far enough to reach the birds. He fell into the water instead, much to his annoyance and much to his friend's amusement.

ACTUAL DESIGN SIZE
9 x 9 in (23 x 23 cm)

MATERIALS
◆ 1 piece of 14-count Zweigart Aida in white measuring approximately 14 x 14 in (35.5 x 35.5 cm)
◆ No. 24 tapestry needle

THREADS

DMC Colour	Metres
white	2
907 lime green	3
400 dark tan	2
972 bright yellow	2
937 sage green	9
906 bright green	12
3776 ginger	3
647 pale grey	7
844 very dark grey	2
775 pale blue	2
722 dull orange	3
720 tan	3
996 pale electric blue	1
995 electric blue	2
3824 pale peach	2
3325 blue	2
677 pale yellow	2
645 dark grey	3
3072 stone	4
310 black	5
606 red	2

INSTRUCTIONS
Mark the centre of the chart. Find the centre of your material and make long tacking stitches across and down to use as your guides. Using two strands of stranded cotton unless otherwise stated (except for backstitching where you use one strand only) begin your work following the chart. For full instructions for cross stitches, backstitches, special shaping stitches, long stitches, lazy daisy stitches and French knots, see the *Techniques* section on pages 125–127.

COLOURS FOR BACKSTITCHING
Backstitch water drops and top edge of bird bath using 775.
Rest of backstitching use 310.

COLOURS FOR LONG STITCHES
Stalks and leaves on flowers use 937.
Grass tufts use 907 (one strand).
Cats' whiskers use white.

LAZY DAISY STITCHES
Flower petals use white.

FRENCH KNOTS
Birds' eyes, cats' whisker dots use 310.
Pupils on wet cat's eyes use white.

Berries in the bush use 606.
Centres of flowers use 972.

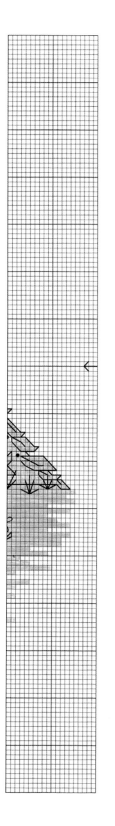

KEY

⊞	White – Wet cat's face, paws, tail
⊞	907 Bush highlights
⊞	400 Stripes on laughing cat
⊞	972 Wet cat's eyes, birds' beaks
⊞	937 Bush
⊞	906 Grass
⊞	3776 Laughing cat
⊞	647 Table and steps
⊞	844 Table shadow
⊞	775 Water and drops
⊞	722 Wet cat
⊞	720 Stripes on wet cat
⊞	996 Birds' faces and chests
⊞	995 Birds
⊞	3824 Inside ears
⊞	3325 Water
⊞	677 Stomach of laughing cat
⊞	645 Rim of table
⊞	3072 Table

Oops! This cat looks very sorry for itself as its little game has backfired slightly.

Hickory, Dickory, Dock

Cats love chasing mice and these cats are patiently watching the mice go round the clock. You could turn this design into a very practical gift for someone by adding a battery-powered clock mechanism, available from craft shops.

ACTUAL DESIGN SIZE:
10 x 8½ in (25.5 x 21.5 cm)

MATERIALS
◆ 1 piece of 14-count Zweigart Aida in cream measuring approximately 15 x 13½ in (38 x 34 cm)
◆ No. 24 tapestry needle

INSTRUCTIONS
Mark the centre of the chart. Find the centre of your material and make long tacking stitches across and down. Using two strands of stranded cotton (except for backstitching where you use one strand only unless otherwise stated) begin your work following the chart. Full instructions for cross stitches, backstitches, special shaping stitches, long stitches and French knots are in the *Techniques* section on pages 125–127.

THREADS

DMC	Metres
310 black	3
white	5
762 very pale grey	3
535 dark grey	6
746 cream	5
725 dark yellow	2
754 peach	1
353 light salmon pink	3
720 tan	5
722 dull orange	5
841 light mink brown	4
3819 pale green	2
606 bright red	2
318 medium grey	1
839 mink brown	5

COLOURS FOR BACKSTITCHING
Backstitch cats using 310.
Backstitch numbers using 606 (two strands).
Backstitch mice using 318.
Backstitch around paw prints using 839.

This perky little cat will brighten any wall that you hang it on.

LONG STITCHES

Whiskers on ginger cat use 746.

Whiskers on grey cat use 762.

Inside cats' ears use 310 (one strand).

FRENCH KNOTS

Paw prints use 839.

All other French knots use 310.

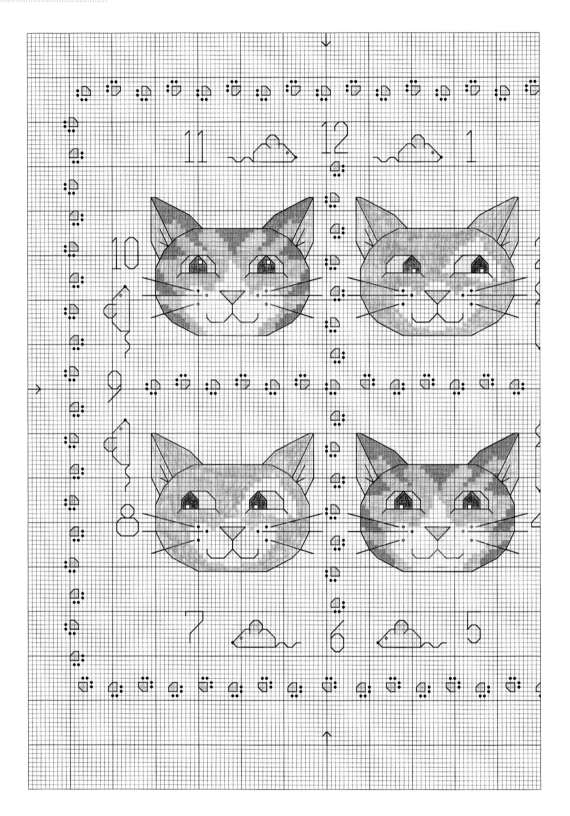

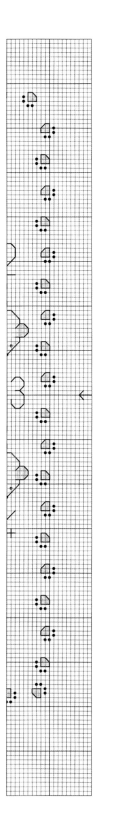

KEY

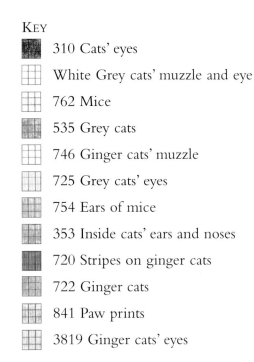

310 Cats' eyes

White Grey cats' muzzle and eye

762 Mice

535 Grey cats

746 Ginger cats' muzzle

725 Grey cats' eyes

754 Ears of mice

353 Inside cats' ears and noses

720 Stripes on ginger cats

722 Ginger cats

841 Paw prints

3819 Ginger cats' eyes

This cat is keeping very still but its eyes are keeping track of the mice around the clock.

Fluffy Faces

These designs can be used to stitch cute and very quick pictures. They can be personalized by using the letters of the alphabet and numbers on page 61. You can make birthday cards, anniversary cards, samplers – the list is endless.

THERE'S A BEE ON MY NOSE!

ACTUAL DESIGN SIZE: 31 x 42 stitches

THREADS

⊞	White
▦	310 black
⊞	353 light salmon pink
⊞	703 green
⊞	747 pale blue

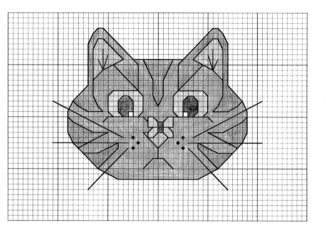

Use 310 for all backstitching and French knots on whisker dots.
Use White (two strands) for whiskers.

HELP!

ACTUAL DESIGN SIZE: 38 x 46 stitches

THREADS
DMC Colour

⊞	White
▦	310 black
⊞	353 light salmon pink
⊞	743 bright yellow

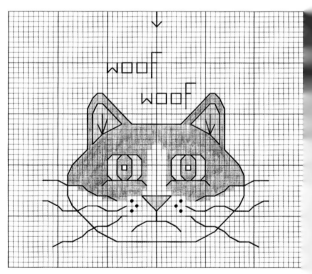

Use 762 very pale grey for backstitching around eyes and whiskers (two strands). Use 310 for rest of backstitching and French knots.

BUZZ BUZZ

ACTUAL DESIGN SIZE:
47 x 47 stitches

THREADS
DMC Colours

	White
	310 black
	353 light salmon pink
	743 bright yellow
	747 pale blue

Use 762 very pale grey for backstitching around eyes and whiskers (two strands). Use 310 for rest of backstitching and French knots on whisker dots.

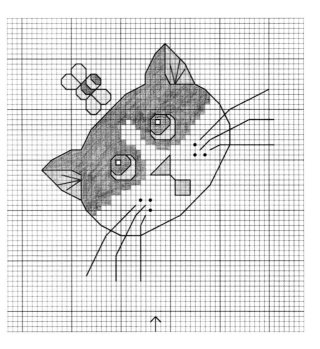

HAPPY CAT

ACTUAL DESIGN SIZE:
47 x 55 stitches

THREADS
DMC Colour

	353 light salmon pink
	720 tan
	722 pale orange

Use White (two strands for cat's whiskers. Use 310 black for all backstitching and French knots on whisker dots.

SMILING CAT

ACTUAL DESIGN SIZE:
33 x 48 stitches

THREADS
DMC Colour

⊞	White
▦	310 black
▦	353 light salmon pink
▦	703 green
▦	720 tan
▦	722 pale orange

Use White (two strands) for whiskers. Use
310 for all backstitching and French knots
on whisker dots.

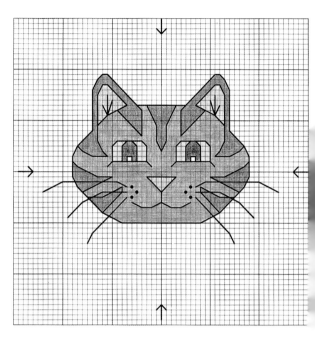

POORLY CAT

ACTUAL DESIGN SIZE:
29 x 44 stitches

THREADS
DMC Colours

⊞	White
▦	310 black
▦	353 light salmon pink
▦	703 green
▦	720 tan
▦	722 pale orange
▦	996 pale electric blue

Use White (two strands) for whiskers. Use
310 for all backstitching and French knots
on whisker dots.

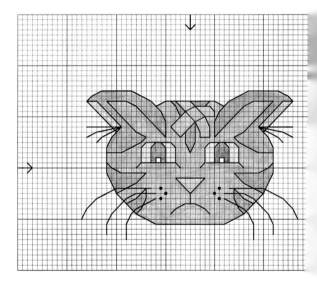

CAT FOR A NEW BABY

ACTUAL DESIGN SIZE:
34 x 44 stitches

THREADS

DMC Colour

	White
	310 black
	353 light salmon pink
	703 green
	720 tan
	722 light orange
	745 pale yellow
	800 light blue
	809 blue
	3708 light pink

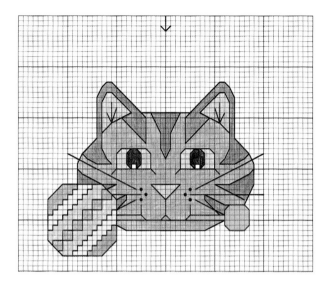

Use White (two strands) for whiskers. Use 310 for all backstitching and French knots on whisker dots.

PARTY TIME CAT

ACTUAL DESIGN SIZE:
33 x 42 stitches

THREADS

DMC Colours

	White
	310 black
	353 light salmon pink
	666 bright red
	743 bright yellow
	762 very pale grey

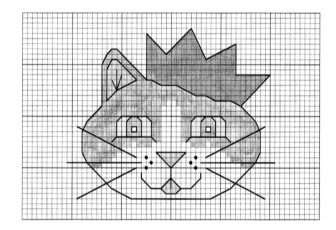

Use 762 for backstitching around eyes and cat's whiskers (two strands). Use 310 for rest of backstitching and French knots on whisker dots.

SOMETHING FISHY!

ACTUAL DESIGN SIZE:
36 x 50 stitches

THREADS
DMC Colour

⊞	White
▦	310 black
▦	353 light salmon pink
▦	743 bright yellow
▦	996 pale electric blue

Use 762 very pale grey for backstitching around eyes and whiskers (two strands). Use 743 for backstitching fish bone. All other backstitching and French knots on whisker dots use 310.

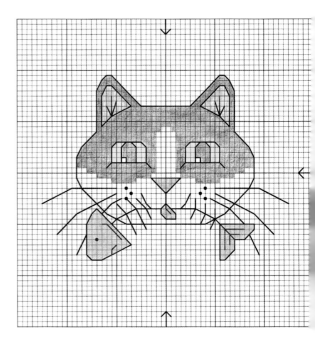

WET CAT

ACTUAL DESIGN SIZE:
28 x 54 stitches

THREADS
DMC Colour

⊞	White
▦	310 black
▦	353 light salmon pink
▦	743 bright yellow
▦	827 light blue

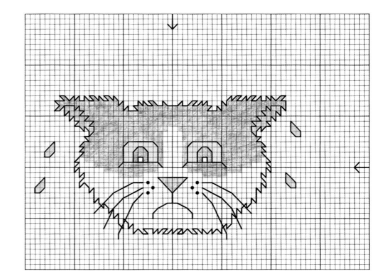

Use 762 very pale grey for backstitching around eyes and whiskers (two strands).

Use 310 for rest of backstitching and French knots on whisker dots.

Alphabet

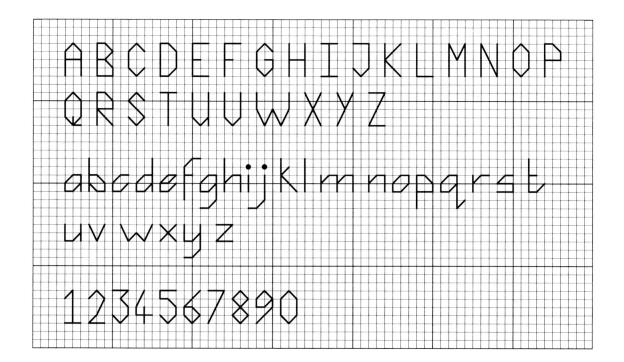

Use these simple backstitch letters and numbers to add a personal touch to the designs on these pages. You can stitch names, dates or mottoes in a colour to match either these cats or the bears on pages 118-122, the mount of a gift card or the taste of whoever the finished piece is intended for.

Washday Bear

I remember my favourite bear being washed and hung outside to dry with the rest of the washing. In this picture he is drip-drying along with the clothes and as he dries, he starts to smile again. A perfect design for the kitchen or bathroom.

ACTUAL DESIGN SIZE:
6 x 11 in (15 x 28 cm)

MATERIALS
◆ 1 piece of 16-count Zweigart Aida in white measuring approximately 11 x 16 in (28 x 40.5 cm)
◆ No. 24 tapestry needle

INSTRUCTIONS
Mark the centre of the chart. Find the centre of your material and make long tacking stitches across and down. Using two strands of stranded cotton (except for backstitching where you use one strand only unless stated otherwise) begin your work. Full instructions for cross stitches, backstitches and special shaping stitches are in the *Techniques* section on pages 125–127.

THREADS

DMC Colour	Metres
3747 pale lilac	5
775 pale blue	1
3824 pale peach	2
976 ginger	3
3823 very pale yellow	2
745 pale yellow	7
436 light brown	4
300 very dark brown	2
321 dull red	1
975 dark brown	2
3827 light ginger	5
666 bright red	1
3826 dark ginger	3
814 maroon	1
435 light brown	1
340 dark lilac	1
3341 peach	1
3325 blue	1
743 bright yellow	1
964 light mint green	1
341 lilac	2

This bear is clean and fluffy now, when dry, he'll be ready to be played with again.

COLOURS FOR BACKSTITCHING

Backstitch all bear using 300.

Backstitch around bow using 814.

Backstitch pegs using 435.

Backstitch pale lilac shorts using 340.

Backstitch yellow washing using 745.

Backstitch bib using 3341.

Backstitch drops of water using 3325.

Backstitch T-shirt seams and fold using 743.

Backstitch alphabet onto the bib using 964 (two strands).

Backstitch washing line using 341 (two strands).

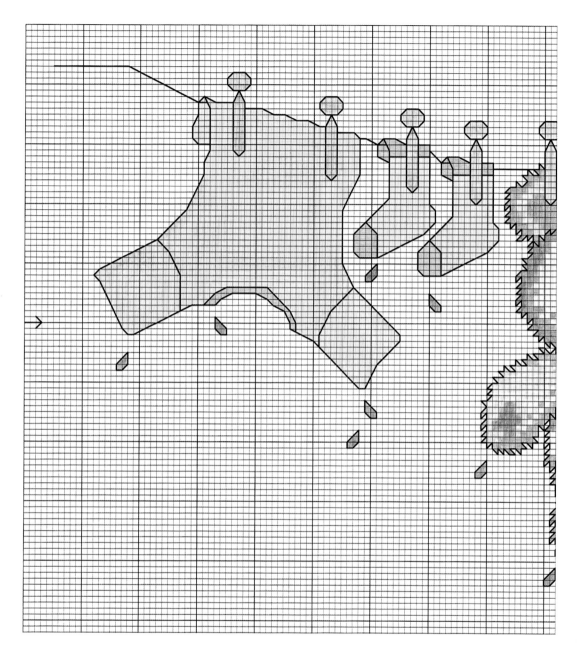

KEY

▦	3747 Shorts, trim on socks, T-shirt	▦	3823 Bib
▦	775 Water drops	▦	745 T-shirt, socks, pocket on shorts
▦	3824 Trim on bib	▦	436 Washing pegs
▦	976 Bear	▦	300 Bear's nose, eyes, shading

 321 Inside bear's bow

975 Foot pads, inside ears, shading

3827 Bear

666 Bear's bow

3826 Bear's paws, shading

Valentine Bear

This is a beautiful design that you could stitch for someone very special. It is full of love and happiness and when I designed this picture I had my husband in mind because this is a special picture for a special person.

ACTUAL DESIGN SIZE:
5 x 9½ in (12.5 x 24 cm)

MATERIALS
✦ 1 piece of 18-count Zweigart in white measuring approximately 10 x 14½ in (25.5 x 37 cm)
✦ No. 24 tapestry needle

INSTRUCTIONS
Mark the centre of the chart. Find the centre of the material and make long tacking stitches across and down. Using two strands of stranded cotton (except for backstitching where you use one strand only) begin your work following the chart.

For full instructions for cross stitches, backstitches and special shaping stitches, see the *Techniques* section on pages 125–127.

THREADS

DMC Colour	Metres
938 very dark brown	1
975 brown	2
3826 dark ginger	2
976 ginger	3
3827 light ginger	5
321 dark red	1
666 bright red	2
891 dark coral	2
3706 coral	1
957 baby pink	1
894 pink	2
963 very light pink	1
605 light pink	1
743 bright yellow	1
745 pale yellow	2
white	1
964 light mint green	2
340 dark lilac	1
300 dark brown	1
958 jade green	1

COLOURS FOR BACKSTITCHING

Backstitch bear's eyes, nose, mouth using 938.

Backstitch rest of bear using 300.

Backstitch around small plain hearts using same colour as the cross stitches.

Backstitch around green and white checked heart using 958.

Backstitch around lilac and pink horizontal-striped heart using 340.

Backstitch around pink and yellow vertical-striped heart using 957.

Backstitch around the green and yellow criss-crossed heart using 964.

Backstitch around yellow and pink spotted heart using 743.

This warm-hearted bear will bring a smile to anyone's face.

KEY

938 Bear's nose

975 Dark shading on bear

3826 Medium shading on bear

976 Light shading on bear

3827 Bear

321 Plain heart

666 Plain heart

891 Plain heart

3706 Spots on spotted heart

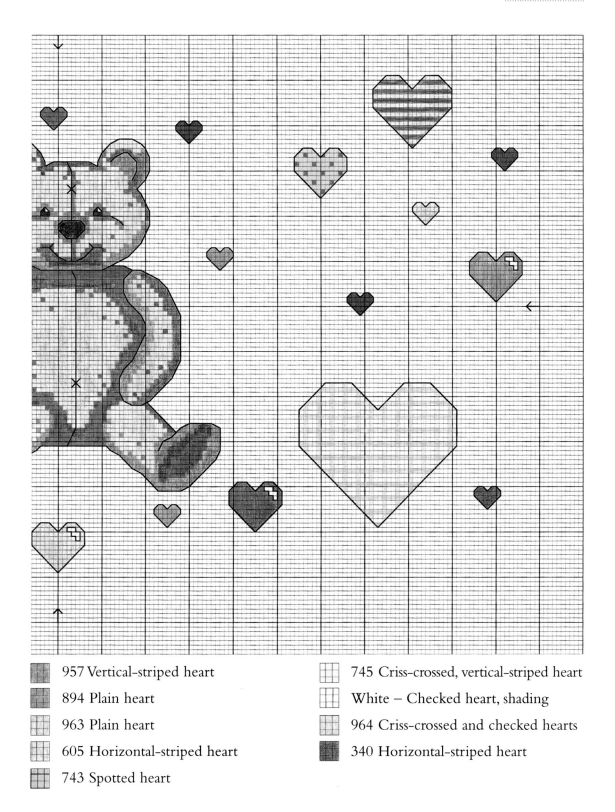

957 Vertical-striped heart		745 Criss-crossed, vertical-striped heart	
894 Plain heart		White – Checked heart, shading	
963 Plain heart		964 Criss-crossed and checked hearts	
605 Horizontal-striped heart		340 Horizontal-striped heart	
743 Spotted heart			

69

Balloon Bear

....

I saw a little girl on the television recently holding a bouquet of flowers, her toes turned in just like this bear, and she also had this very shy expression on her face. I think our little bear also has a real surprise for some lucky person! I have mounted this design onto a flexi-hoop (see Techniques *section for instructions), but you could stitch this onto a shirt or fray the edges of your fabric and make a wall hanging.*

ACTUAL DESIGN SIZE:
4 x 2¼ in (10 x 5.5 cm)

MATERIALS
✦ 1 piece of 18-count Zweigart Aida in white measuring approximately 9 x 7¼ in (23 x 18.5 cm)
✦ No. 24 tapestry needle
✦ Flexi-hoop (optional)

INSTRUCTIONS
Mark the centre of the chart. Find the centre of your material and make long tacking stitches across and down. Using two strands of stranded cotton (except for backstitching where you stitch with one strand only) begin your work following the chart. Full instructions for cross stitches, backstitches, special shaping stitches, lazy daisy stitches and French knots are in the *Techniques* section on pages 125–127.

THREADS

DMC Colour	Metres
906 bright green	2
996 pale electric blue	1
606 red	1
973 bright yellow	1
433 medium brown	2
435 light brown	2
437 beige	3
898 very dark brown	1
701 green	1

COLOURS FOR BACKSTITCHING
Backstitch around each balloon using the same colour as the balloon.
Backstitching on the bear using 433.
Backstitch bear's mouth and nose using 898.
Backstitch string of the red balloon using 433.

COLOURS FOR LONG STITCHES
Stalks of the flowers use 701.

LAZY DAISY STITCHES
Flower petals use 973 (two strands).
Leaves of flowers use 701
(two strands).

FRENCH KNOTS
Centres of flowers use 606.
Bear's eyes use 898.

This bashful-looking bear is waiting to surprise someone with a bunch of cheerful, brightly coloured balloons

KEY

	906 Grass
	996 Blue balloon
	606 Red balloon
	973 Yellow balloon
	433 Inside ears
	435 Shading on bear
	437 Bear
	898 Bear's nose

Pen Pal

....

I love writing letters and sending cards to people and I designed this little bear with that in mind. Again this project can be framed or, as I have done, mounted in a gift card. This is a quick picture to make which can be also stitched onto any item of clothing or pillowslip using waste canvas (see Techniques section).

ACTUAL DESIGN SIZE:
2¾ x 3¾ in (7 x 9.5 cm)

MATERIALS
◆ 1 piece of 18-count Zweigart Aida in white measuring approximately 7¾ x 8¾ in (19.5 x 22 cm)
◆ No. 24 tapestry needle
◆ Gift card and envelope (optional)

INSTRUCTIONS
Mark the centre of the chart. Find the centre of your material and make long tacking stitches across and down. Using two strands of stranded cotton (except for backstitching where you use one strand only) begin your work following the chart. Full instructions for cross stitches, backstitches, special shaping stitches, long stitches, lazy daisy stitches and French knots are in the *Techniques* section on pages 125–127. Instructions on how to mount your work into a gift card can also be found in the *Techniques* section.

THREADS

DMC Colour	Metres
606 red	1
972 bright yellow	1
437 beige	2
435 light brown	2
747 pale blue	2
3823 very pale yellow	1
906 bright green	4
898 very dark brown	1
434 brown	1
433 medium brown	1
3766 blue	1
701 green	1

COLOURS FOR BACKSTITCHING
Backstitch bear's nose and mouth using 898.
Backstitch butterflies' bodies, antennae and writing on the paper using 898.
Backstitch rest of bear using 433.
Backstitch feather using 3766.
Backstitch paper using 435.

Backstitch butterflies' wings using 606.
Backstitch dots on the butterflies wings
using 972.

FRENCH KNOTS
Bear's eye use 898.
Flowers use 972.

LONG STITCHES
Stalks of the flowers use 701.

LAZY DAISY STITCHES
Flower petals use 3823.
Leaves on flowers use 701.

This bear is relaxing in the sun, and with the help of the butterflies, is writing a long letter to an old friend.

KEY

- 606 Butterflies' wings
- 972 Spots on butterflies
- 437 Bear
- 435 Shading on bear
- 747 Feather
- 3823 Paper
- 906 Grass
- 898 Butterflies' bodies, nose and eye of bear
- 434 Ears and bottom of paws

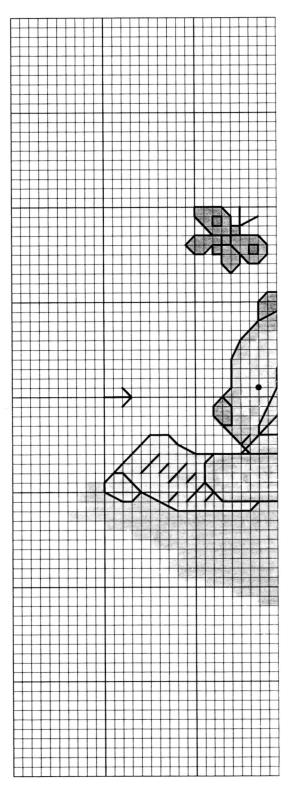

Birthday Sampler

A complete record of a child's birth in which you can stitch the name, date of birth, weight and length of the baby would make the perfect present for a new-born boy or girl. There is a backstitch alphabet on pages 82–83 to help you to stitch all these details. The colours are very soft and gentle, which I think are appropriate for such a young arrival – I have chosen to stitch this design in pink but, of course, you can choose your own colours for the baby's details and bows.

ACTUAL DESIGN SIZE:
12½ x 9¾ in (32 x 25 cm)

MATERIALS
◆ 1 piece of 14-count Zweigart Aida in white measuring approximately
17½ x 14¾ in (44 x 37 cm)
◆ No. 24 tapestry needle

INSTRUCTIONS
Mark the centre of the chart. Find the centre of your material and make long tacking stitches across and down. Using two strands of stranded cotton (except for backstitching where you use one strand only) begin your work following the chart. Full instructions for cross stitches, backstitches, special shaping stitches and French knots are in the *Techniques* section on pages 125–127.

THREADS

DMC Colour	Metres
3706 pink	2
745 pale yellow	3
340 lilac	2
3747 pale lilac	3
3708 light pink	5
809 blue	2
801 dark brown	2
434 brown	3
959 mint green	6
436 light brown	6
800 light blue	3
738 dark beige	6
3746 dark lilac	2
743 bright yellow	2
3705 bright pink	3

COLOURS FOR BACKSTITCHING
Backstitch paws and the bows on the bears using 3746.
Backstitch rest of the bears using 801.

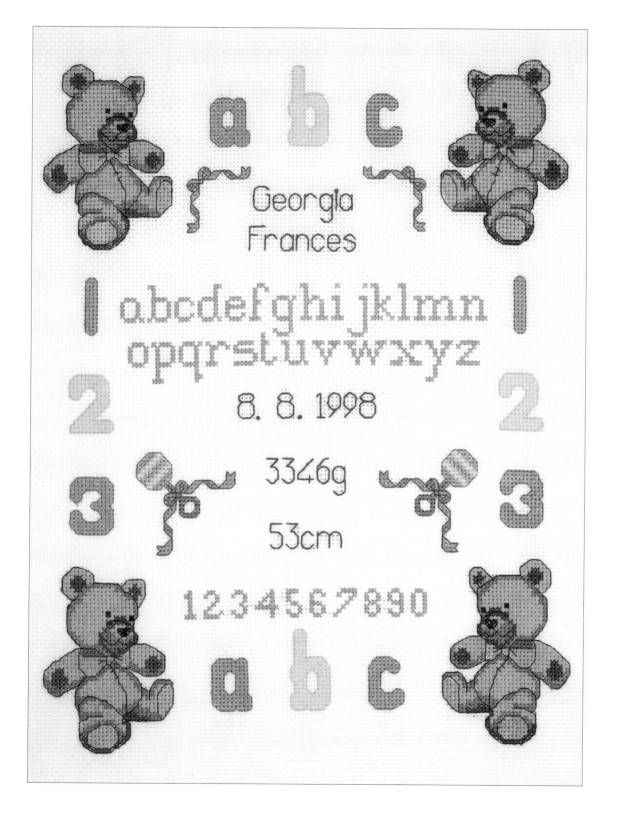

Backstitch around pink numbers and letters in border using 3706.
Backstitch around yellow numbers and letters in border using 743.
Backstitch around blue numbers and letters in border using 809.
Backstitch ribbons using 3705.
Backstitch rattle handles using 809.
Backstitch rattle head using 3706.
Backstitch the baby's details using two strands in the colour of your choice.

FRENCH KNOTS

French knots for the baby's details should be stitched in the colour of your choice.

KEY

- 3706 Dark shading on ribbons
- 745 Yellow letters and rattle
- 340 Inside bow tie
- 3747 Patches on feet and bow tie
- 3708 Pink letters and numbers and light pink on rattles
- 809 Rattle handles
- 801 Bears' eyes and noses
- 434 Paw pads, ears and dark shading
- 459 Central alphabet and numbers
- 436 Bears' light shading
- 800 Letters, rattle and numbers
- 738 Bears

Celebrate a new birth with the help of four captivating bears with blue, or pink, bows.

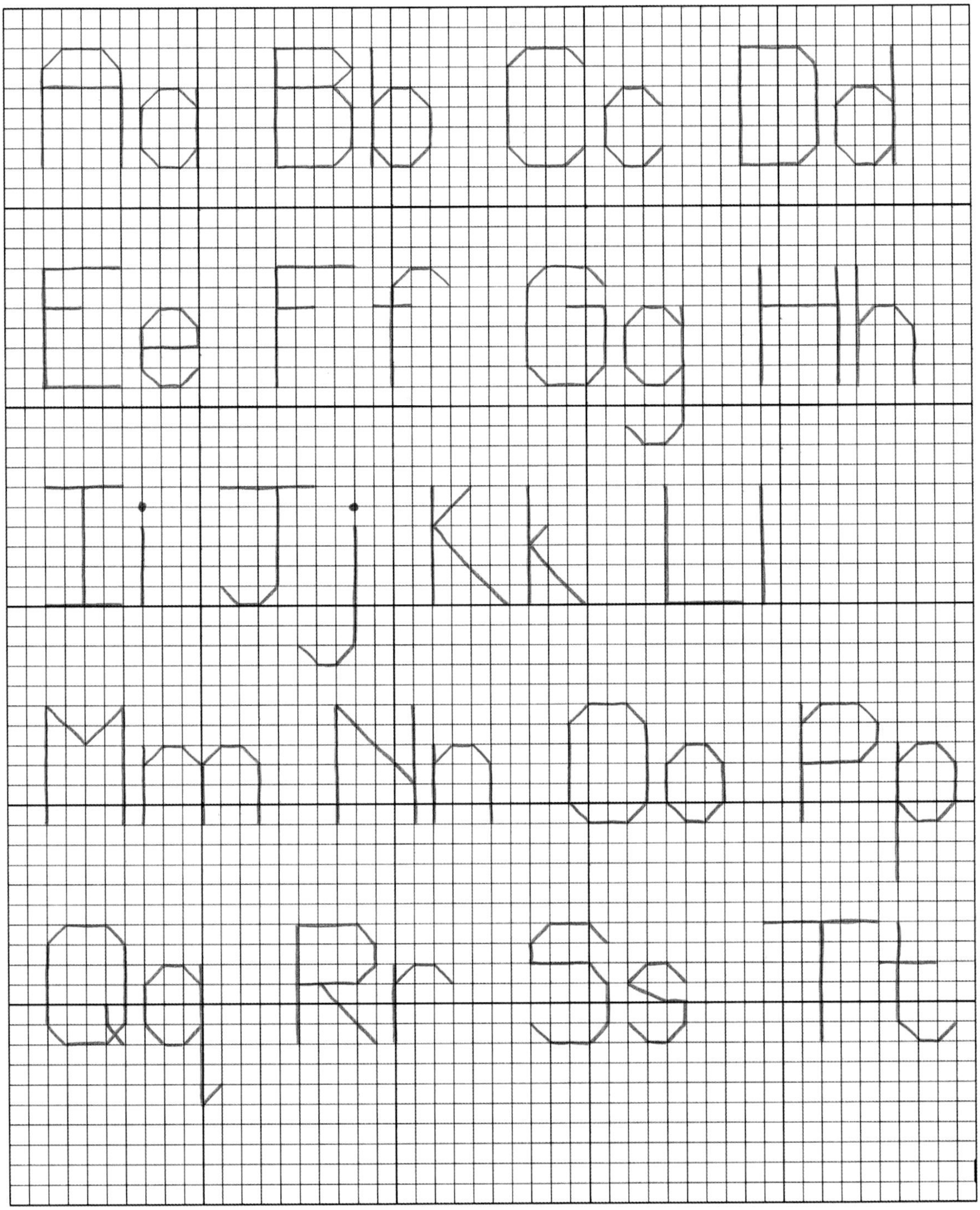

Aa Bb Cc Dd

Ee Ff Gg Hh

Ii Jj Kk Ll

Mm Nn Oo Pp

Qq Rr Ss Tt

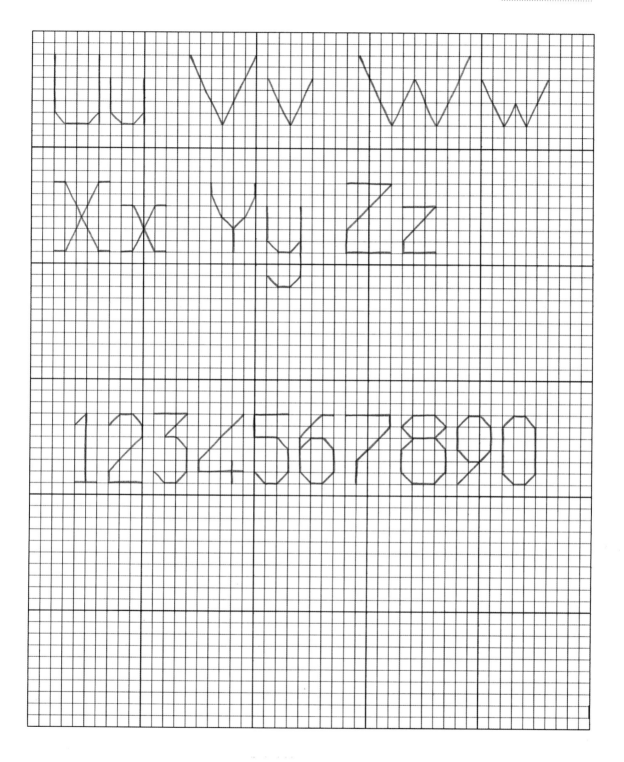

Beau Bear

I love and collect small trinket boxes and I designed this lovely bear to fit inside one. Doesn't he look handsome with his big red bow and wide smile? This design could also be adapted for putting on a dressing table mirror or a brush or it could even be mounted in a gift card.

ACTUAL DESIGN SIZE:
2½ x 2¼ in (6 x 5.5 cm)

MATERIALS
◆ 1 piece of 16-count Zweigart Aida measuring approximately 7½ x 7¼ in (19 x 18.5 cm)
◆ No. 24 tapestry needle
◆ Trinket box (optional)

INSTRUCTIONS
Mark the centre of the chart. Find the centre of your material and make long tacking stitches across and down. Using two strands of stranded cotton (except for backstitching where you use one strand only) begin your work following the chart. For full instructions for cross stitches, backstitches, special shaping stitches and French knots, see the *Techniques* section on pages 125–127. Make up the trinket box following the manufacturer's instructions.

THREADS

DMC Colour	Metres
321 dull red	1
666 bright red	1
938 very dark brown	1
433 medium brown	2
435 light brown	2
437 beige	2
791 royal blue	1

COLOURS FOR BACKSTITCHING
Backstitch bear using 938.
Backstitch around bow using 321.
Backstitch checks on bow using 791.

FRENCH KNOTS
Bear's eyes use 938.

This bear has taken the time this morning to tie a dapper bow.

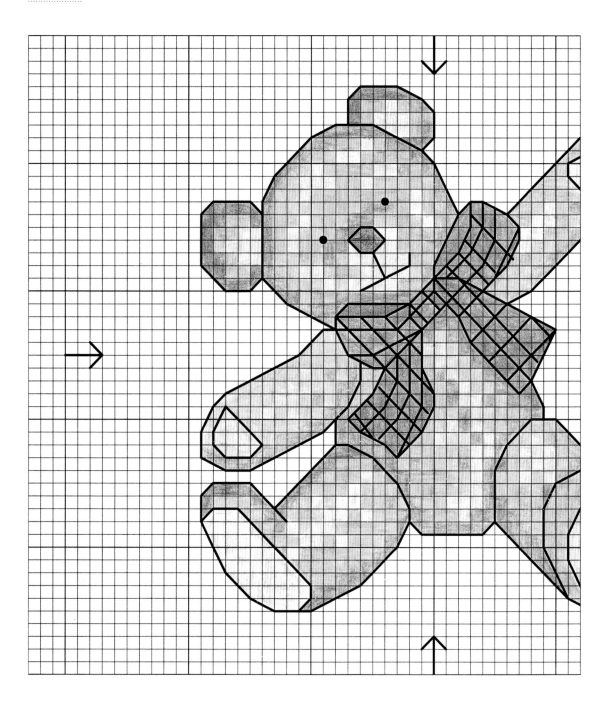

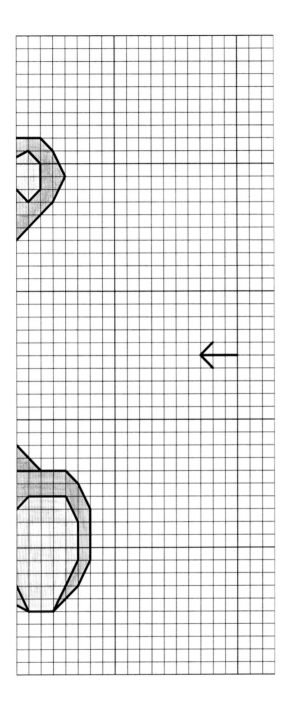

KEY

321 Inside bow

666 Bow

938 Nose

433 Dark colour on bear

435 Medium colour on bear

437 Light colour on bear

The Slipper Fits

A perfect fit! This bear looks very content and snug inside the slipper. My daughter used to play with her bears and she would put them in shoes or slippers to sit them up, which is where the idea for this cute design came from.

ACTUAL DESIGN SIZE:
5 x 6¼ in (12.5 x 16 cm)

MATERIALS
✦ 1 piece of 14-count Zweigart Aida in cream measuring approximately 10 x 11¼ in (25.5 x 29 cm)
✦ No. 24 tapestry needle

INSTRUCTIONS
Mark the centre of the chart. Find the centre of your material and make long tacking stitches across and down. Using two strands of stranded cotton (except for backstitching where you use one strand only) begin your work following the chart. Full instructions for cross stitches, backstitches, special shaping stitches and long stitches are in the *Techniques* section on pages 125–127.

THREADS

DMC Colour	Metres
676 pale mustard	2
898 very dark brown	1
3345 light bottle green	8
890 bottle green	1
606 red	2
817 dark red	1
435 light brown	2
437 beige	3
433 medium brown	2
680 french mustard	1
742 light orange	2
947 orange	2

A slipper left on the floor makes the perfect home for a bear looking for somewhere to play.

COLOURS FOR BACKSTITCHING
Backstitch bear using 898
Backstitch bear's bow using 606
Backstitch sole of slipper using 680.
Backstitch rest of slipper using 890.

LONG STITCHES
Horizontal lines on slipper use 742.
Vertical lines on slipper use 947.

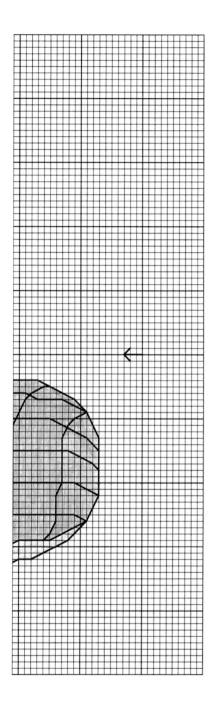

KEY

	676 Slipper sole
	898 Bear's eyes and nose
	3345 Slipper
	890 Slipper trim
	606 Bear's bow
	817 Inside bow
	435 Light shading on bear
	437 Bear
	433 Dark shading on bear

Good Night, Sleep Tight

I love this bear, he looks so dreamy as he floats gently on the clouds looking at the moon and stars. This picture came to me as I was flying back from a holiday and I saw these beautiful fluffy clouds drifting by. It is the type of picture that would look lovely in any bedroom or on a pillowslip, duvet cover or blanket, using waste canvas to transfer the design (see Techniques *section for instructions).*

ACTUAL DESIGN SIZE:
7½ x 8½ in (19 x 21.5 cm)

MATERIALS
◆ 1 piece 32-count Belfast Linen in white measuring approximately 12½ x 13½ in (32 x 34 cm)
◆ No. 24 tapestry needle

INSTRUCTIONS
Mark the centre of the chart. Find the centre of your material and make long tacking stitches across and down. Using two strands of stranded cotton (except for backstitching where you use one strand only – you can, of course, use two strands if you wish but remember to double up on the above quantities of thread required), begin your work following the chart. Full instructions for cross stitches, backstitches, special shaping stitches and French knots are in the *Techniques* section on pages 125–127.

Surrounded by stars and sitting on soft clouds, this little bear will have happy dreams.

| 959 mint green | 2 |
| 3708 bright pink | 2 |

COLOURS FOR BACKSTITCHING
Backstitch around bear using 300.
Bear's nose and mouth using 938.
Backstitch around stars and moon using 972.
Backstitch around blue cloud using 813.
Backstitch around green cloud using 959.
Backstitch around pink cloud using 3708.

FRENCH KNOTS
Bear's eyes use 938.

THREADS

DMC Colour	Metres
938 very dark brown	1
400 chestnut brown	4
3776 tan	5
402 light tan	2
964 light mint green	2
963 pink	2
3824 pale peach	1
827 light blue	2
744 yellow	2
300 dark brown	1
972 bright yellow	2
813 blue	1

KEY

- 938 Bear's nose
- 400 Shading on bear
- 3776 Bear
- 402 Highlights on bear
- 964 Turquoise cloud
- 963 Pink cloud
- 3824 Inside bear's ear
- 827 Blue cloud
- 744 Moon and stars

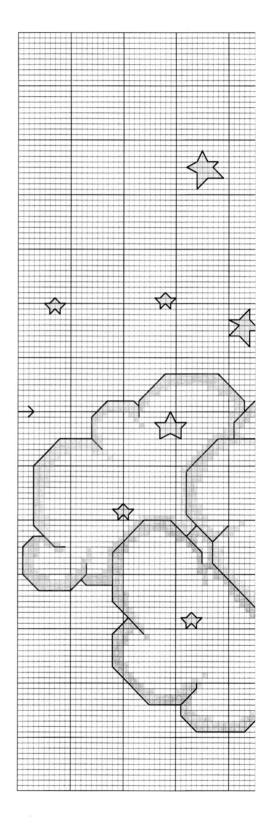

Parlour Bears

This design is similar to a greetings card I found a few years ago. The Victorian bears are so innocent and appealing and I particularly like the way in which they are sitting against a backdrop of Victorian-style wallpaper. I have stitched this design using one strand of stranded cotton, but if you wish to use two strands remember to double up on the thread quantities given below.

ACTUAL DESIGN SIZE:
8 x 7 in (20 x 18 cm)

MATERIALS
◆ 1 piece of 16-count Zweigart Aida in white measuring approximately
13 x 12 in (33 x 31 cm)
◆ No. 24 tapestry needle

INSTRUCTIONS
Mark the centre of the chart. Find the centre of your material and make long

Baby bear is tucked in front of his mother where she can keep an eye on him.

tacking stitches across and down. Using one strand only for all cross stitches and backstitching begin your work following the chart. Full instructions for cross stitches, backstitches, special shaping stitches and half-cross stitches are in the *Techniques* section on pages 125–127.

THREADS

DMC Colour	Metres
301 cinnamon	3
311 royal blue	1
315 grape	2
316 light grape	2
400 chestnut brown	2
420 medium brown	3
422 light mustard	2
435 golden brown	3
436 light golden brown	2
437 camel	2
676 straw yellow	2
677 light straw yellow	2
738 light camel	1
760 rose pink	2
761 pink	2
780 dark golden brown	1
838 dark chocolate brown	1

869 dark khaki brown	2	
3045 light khaki brown	1	
3052 green	3	
3362 dark green	2	
3364 light green	1	
3776 tan	2	
3809 turquoise	1	
3828 mustard	1	

COLOURS FOR BACKSTITCHING

Backstitch bears' mouths using 838.

Backstitch green flower stems using 3052.

HALF-CROSS STITCHES

Shading on floor use 3052.

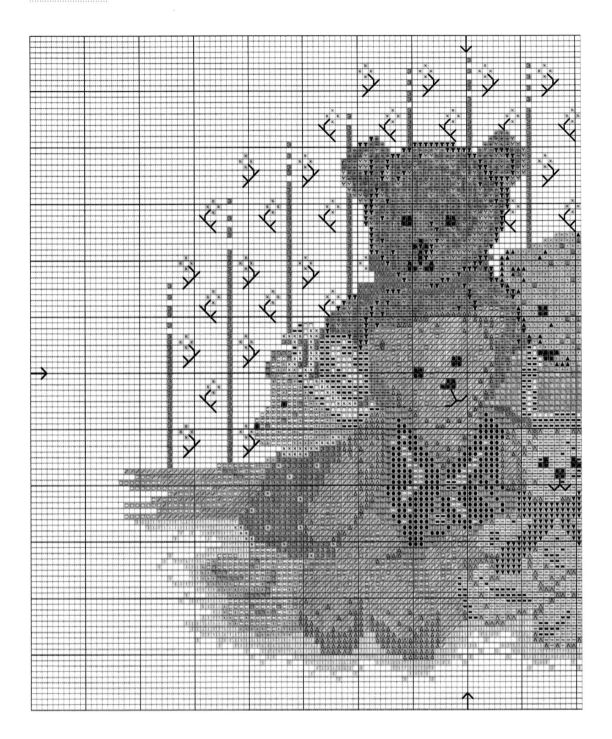

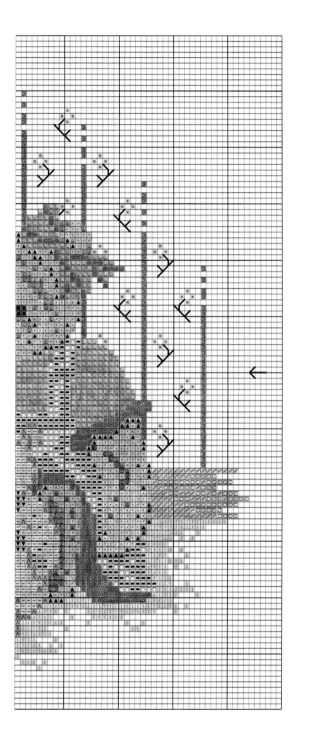
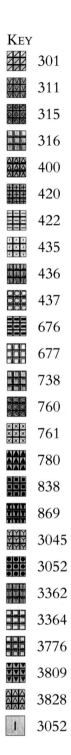

KEY

	301
	311
	315
	316
	400
	420
	422
	435
	436
	437
	676
	677
	738
	760
	761
	780
	838
	869
	3045
	3052
	3362
	3364
	3776
	3809
	3828
	3052

Bear Alphabet

··

This is a delightful and versatile cross-stitch project that can be used to create your name, your child's name or any name you wish. Each letter of this alphabet is, of course, adorned with a smiling bear but the blue and the pink colours of the letters are suggestions only and you can adapt the design very easily. In fact, you could create your own design using graph paper but remember to leave approximately 2 in (6.5 cm) each side of your design for stretching and framing.

ACTUAL DESIGN SIZE OF 'JACK':
3 x 10½ in (7.5 x 27 cm)

MATERIALS USED IN 'JACK'
◆ 1 piece of 14-count Zweigart Aida in white measuring approximately 8 x 15½ in (20 x 39 cm)
◆ No. 24 tapestry needle

INSTRUCTIONS
Mark the centre of the chart. Find the centre of your material and make long tacking stitches across and down. Using two strands of stranded cotton (except for backstitching where you use one strand only) begin your work following the chart. For full instructions for cross stitches, backstitches and special shaping stitches, see the *Techniques* section on pages 125–127.

THREADS USED FOR EACH BEAR

DMC Colour	Metres
898 very dark brown	1
434 brown	1
435 light brown	1
437 beige	3
739 cream	1
761 pink	1
433 medium brown	1

COLOURS FOR BACKSTITCHING BEAR

Backstitch bear's eyes, nose and mouth using 898.

Backstitch bear's muzzle, ears, seams, centre of tummy and lines under eyes using 433.

SUGGESTED COLOURS FOR LETTERING:
(APPROX 3 METRES PER LETTER)

Cross stitch using 996 pale electric blue.
Backstitch using 995 electric blue.
OR **Cross stitch** using 894 pink.
Backstitch using 893 deep pink.

This teddy bear peers out from its letter as it helps to spell out your name.

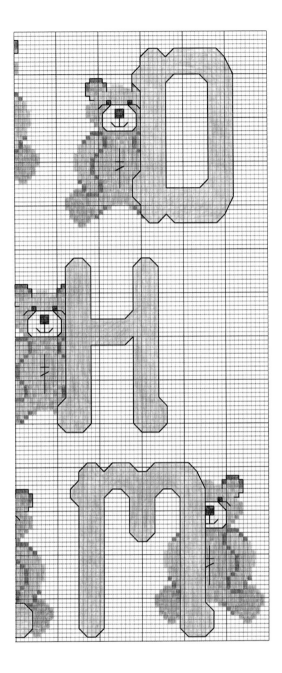

KEY

▦	898 Eyes and nose
▦	434 Top of ears, shading on arms
▦	435 Shading around face, legs, paws
▦	437 Bear
▦	739 Muzzle
▦	761 Paw pads and inside ears

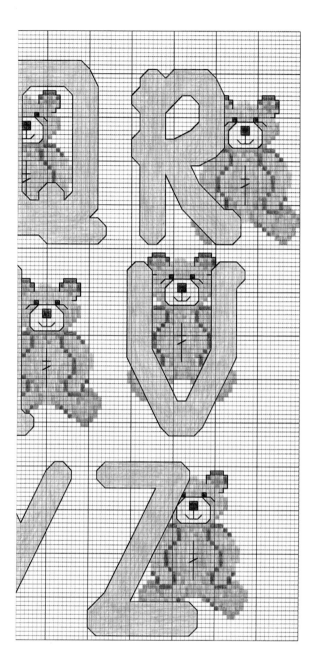

KEY

■ 898 Eyes and nose

■ 434 Top of ears, shading on arms

▦ 435 Shading around face, legs, paws

▦ 437 Bear

□ 739 Muzzle

▦ 761 Paw pads and inside ears

Bears in the Bathroom

Every bathroom should have this picture on the wall. Set in a Victorian-style bathroom, there is one innocent bear reading on the floor and the other, well, what can I say? He's puzzled, I think, as to how he got himself into that situation in the first place. I have stitched this design using one strand of stranded cotton, but if you wish to use two strands, remember to double up on the thread quantities given below.

ACTUAL DESIGN SIZE:
8½ x 8 in (21.5 x 20 cm)

MATERIALS
◆ 1 piece of 16-count Zweigart Aida in white measuring approximately 13½ x 13 in (34 x 33 cm)
◆ No. 24 tapestry needle

INSTRUCTIONS
Mark the centre of the chart. Find the centre of your material and make long tacking stitches across and down. Using one strand only of stranded cotton for cross stitches, backstitching and long stitches unless otherwise stated begin your work following the chart. Full instructions for cross stitches, backstitches, special shaping stitches, long stitches and French knots are in the *Techniques* section on pages 125–127

THREADS

DMC Colour	Metres
301 dark ginger	5
402 light tan	2
433 medium brown	2
666 bright red	1
745 pale yellow	4
798 dark blue	2
800 light blue	9
809 blue	3
898 very dark brown	2
975 dark brown	2
976 ginger	2
3341 peach	1
3776 tan	3
3823 very pale yellow	9
743 bright yellow	2

COLOURS USED FOR BACKSTITCHING
Backstitch decoration on toilet, cistern and toilet chain handle using 798.
Backstitch toilet, toilet paper and around toilet chain handle using 743.
Backstitch bear's mouths and toilet seat using 898.

LONG STITCHES
Toilet chain use 2 strands of 800 (this is one long stitch).
Long continuous lines on floorboards use 898.
Shading on floorboards use 433.

FRENCH KNOTS

For decoration on toilet and cistern
use 798.

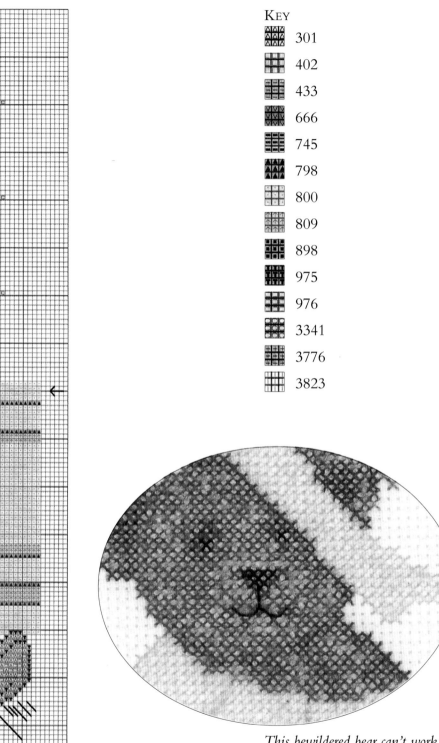

KEY

	301
	402
	433
	666
	745
	798
	800
	809
	898
	975
	976
	3341
	3776
	3823

This bewildered bear can't work out how he managed to entangle himself like this.

Bears in the Park

Surrounded by bushes and flowers these two bears sit and watch the world go by, telling stories to each other and enjoying their surroundings, while the butterflies eavesdrop. This picture reminds me of when my children were small and we used to sit on the park bench and watch the butterflies on a warm summer's day.

ACTUAL DESIGN SIZE:
6½ x 11¼ in (16.5 x 29 cm)

MATERIALS
◆ 1 piece of 14-count Zweigart Aida in cream measuring approximately 11½ x 16¼ in (29 x 41 cm)
◆ No. 24 tapestry needle

THREADS

DMC Colour	Metres
413 dark grey	3
433 medium brown	3
435 light brown	3
702 medium green	9
704 light green	6
973 bright yellow	1
3776 tan	10
340 dark lilac	1
666 bright red	1
995 electric blue	1
957 baby pink	1
437 beige	5
543 pale beige	1
838 dark chocolate brown	1
898 very dark brown	2
841 light mink brown	2
839 mink brown	2
3823 very pale yellow	1
310 black	4
701 green	1

INSTRUCTIONS
Mark the centre of the chart. Find the centre of your material and make long tacking stitches across and down. Using two strands of stranded cotton (except for backstitching where you use one strand only) begin your work following the chart. For full instructions for cross stitches, backstitches, special shaping stitches and long stitches, see the *Techniques* section on pages 125–127.

COLOURS FOR BACKSTITCHING
Backstitch big bear using 898.
Backstitch small bear using 838.
All other backstitching use 310.

LONG STITCHES
Tufts of grass use 701.

These two friends meet every week on this bench in the park to catch up on each other's news and plan the next week's fun and games.

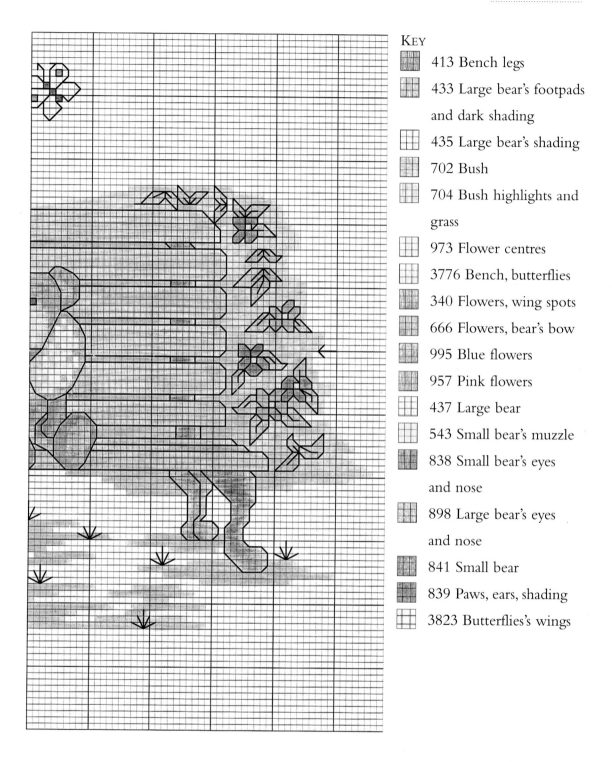

KEY

▦ 413 Bench legs

▦ 433 Large bear's footpads and dark shading

▦ 435 Large bear's shading

▦ 702 Bush

▦ 704 Bush highlights and grass

▦ 973 Flower centres

▦ 3776 Bench, butterflies

▦ 340 Flowers, wing spots

▦ 666 Flowers, bear's bow

▦ 995 Blue flowers

▦ 957 Pink flowers

▦ 437 Large bear

▦ 543 Small bear's muzzle

▦ 838 Small bear's eyes and nose

▦ 898 Large bear's eyes and nose

▦ 841 Small bear

▦ 839 Paws, ears, shading

▦ 3823 Butterflies's wings

Nursery Bears

When I was in London, I visited the toy department of a large department store. It was there that I saw this beautiful rocking horse surrounded by numerous teddy bears and thought that if I were a young child again, how much I would enjoy playing with these toys. This picture reflects such a childhood and would look perfect on the wall of a playroom or nursery. I have stitched this design using one strand of stranded cotton, but if you wish to use two strands remember to double up on the thread quantities.

ACTUAL DESIGN SIZE
11½ x 9 in (29 x 23 cm)

MATERIALS
◆ 1 piece of 16-count Zweigart Aida in white measuring approximately 16½ x 14 in (42 x 36 cm)
◆ No. 24 tapestry needle

INSTRUCTIONS
Mark the centre of the chart. Find the centre of your material and make long tacking stitches across and down. Using one strand only of stranded cotton begin your work following the chart. Full instructions for cross stitches, backstitches, special shaping stitches, half-cross stitches and lazy daisy stitches are in the *Techniques* section on pages 125–127.

THREADS

DMC Colour	Metres
301 cinnamon	2
310 black	1
312 dark blue	1
318 medium grey	2
322 mid blue	1
335 dark pink	2
413 dark grey	2
414 light grey	1
415 very pale grey	2
433 medium brown	1
434 brown	2
435 light brown	2
436 light golden brown	3
437 beige	4
666 bright red	1
712 cream	1
738 dark beige	1
744 yellow	2
745 pale yellow	1
762 very pale silver grey	4
838 dark chocolate brown	1
839 dark mink brown	1
840 mink brown	2
841 light mink brown	2
899 pink	2
975 dark brown	2
3325 light blue	2
3326 light pink	2
3755 blue	5
3816 green	2
3817 light green	3
white	1
3777 damson	4

COLOURS FOR BACKSTITCHING
Backstitch bear's mouths using 838.
Backstitch panelling using 3777.

HALF-CROSS STITCHES
For the panel shading use 3777.

LAZY DAISY STITCHES
Lazy daisy stitches on yellow collar of pink dress use 335. Refer to finished picture for positioning of stitches.

KEY

▲▲▲	301
▦	310
▨	312
▩	318
▦	322
▲▲▲	335
▦	413
▦	414
▦	415
Ⅴ Ⅴ Ⅴ	433
● ●	434
Ⅴ Ⅴ Ⅴ	435
▦	436
▼▼▼	437
✕✕✕	666
▦	712
▦	738
▦	744
▦	745
▦	762
▦	838
▦	839
▦	840
S S S	841
▦	899
▨	975
▦	3325
▦	3326

▲▲▲	3755
▦	3816
▦	3817
▦	White
▽	3777

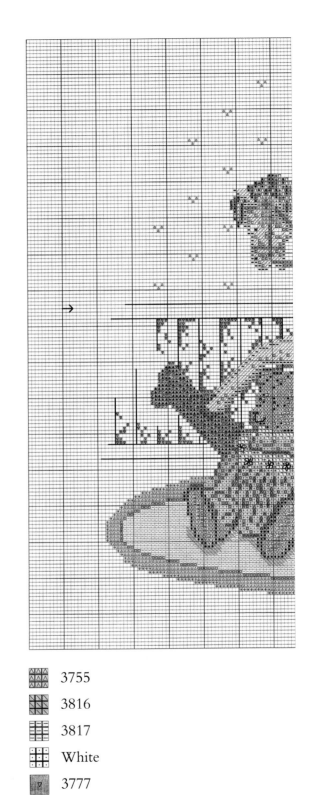

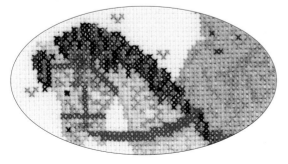

The nursery bears take it in turns to ride on this magnificent rocking horse with its flowing mane and bright red bridle.

Furry Faces

The following bear faces can be used to design simple yet adorable pictures. They can be given a personal touch by the addition of the letters of the alphabet and numbers provided on page 61 and just like the cat heads, you can turn them into a variety of gifts – trinket boxes or transfer them onto clothing or bed linen using waste canvas.

PARTY BEAR

ACTUAL DESIGN SIZE:
33 x 37 stitches

THREADS
DMC Colour
- 606 red
- 3824 pale peach
- 801 dark brown
- 434 brown
- 436 light brown

Use 801 for all backstitching.

SHY BEAR

ACTUAL DESIGN SIZE:
39 x 40 stitches

THREADS
DMC Colour
- 436 light brown
- 437 beige
- 801 dark brown
- 3824 pale peach

Use 801 for all backstitching.

BUBBLE BEAR

ACTUAL DESIGN SIZE:
47 x 48 stitches

THREADS
DMC Colour

- 435 light brown
- 437 beige
- 747 pale blue
- 801 dark brown
- 827 light blue
- 828 very light blue
- 3824 pale peach
- White

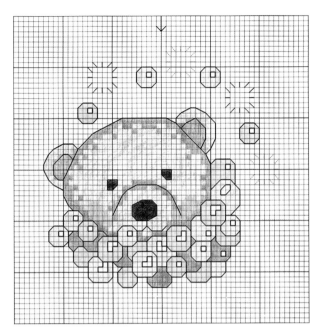

Use 801 blue for backstitching bear. Use
809 for backstitching whole bubbles and
bold dotted lines (burst bubbles).
Use 827 for backstitching faint dotted
lines (burst bubbles).

BEAR PEEPING OVER WALL

ACTUAL DESIGN SIZE: 30 x 34 stitches

THREADS
DMC Colour

- 720 tan
- 3824 pale peach
- 3826 dark ginger
- 3827 light ginger
- 801 dark brown

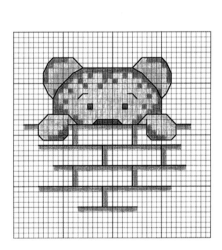

Use 801 for all backstitching.

Grandmother Bear

Actual Design Size:
41 stitches x 31 stitches

Threads
DMC Colour
- 699 emerald green
- 783 mustard yellow
- 797 royal blue
- 800 light blue
- 938 very dark brown
- 975 dark brown
- 3823 very pale yellow
- 3826 dark ginger

Use 801 dark brown for all backstitching.

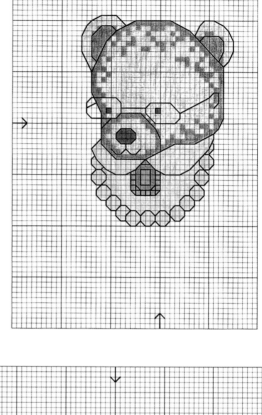

Flower Bear

Actual Design Size:
35 stitches x 42 stitches

Threads
DMC Colour
- 435 light brown
- 437 beige
- 726 yellow
- 801 dark brown
- 891 coral
- 905 green
- 907 lime green
- 996 pale electric blue
- 3824 pale peach

Use 801 for all backstitching.

BIRTH ANNOUNCEMENT BEAR

ACTUAL DESIGN SIZE
(excluding any writing):
32 stitches x 32 stitches

THREADS
DMC Colour

- 435 light brown
- 437 beige
- 761 pink
- 898 very dark brown

Boy's Bow:
- 800 light blue
- 809 blue

Girl's Bow:
- 956 bright pink
- 957 pink

Use 801 dark brown for all backstitching.

GET WELL SOON BEAR

ACTUAL DESIGN SIZE:
37 stitches x 34 stitches

THREADS
DMC Colour

- 745 pale yellow
- 946 orange
- 801 dark brown
- 975 brown
- 3776 tan
- 3325 blue

Use 801 for all backstitching.

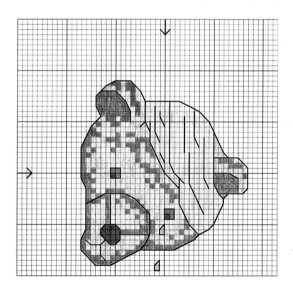

SWEETHEART BEAR

ACTUAL DESIGN SIZE:
28 stitches x 34 stitches

THREADS
DMC Colour
- 434 brown
- 435 light brown
- 437 beige
- 739 cream
- 761 pink
- 606 red
- 898 very dark brown

Use 801 dark brown for all backstitching.

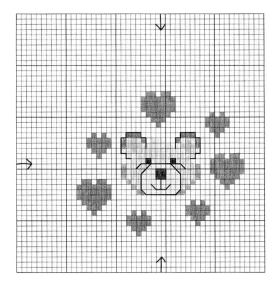

CHRISTMAS BEAR

ACTUAL DESIGN SIZE
(excluding any writing):
25 stitches x 39 stitches

THREADS
DMC Colour
- 666 bright red
- 801 dark brown
- 3824 pale peach
- 3826 dark ginger
- 977 golden tan
- White

Use 801 for all backstitching.

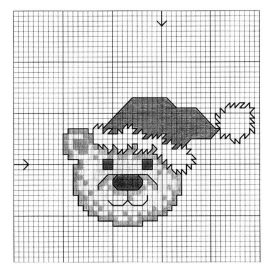

Techniques

TIPS

◆ Always work with clean hands.

◆ Do not drag threads across spaces where there are no cross stitches, this will show up when the picture is stretched.

◆ Let the needle hang regularly to avoid twisting the thread.

◆ Take the work out of the embroidery hoop at night or when you stop working to avoid marking the fabric.

◆ Attach your needle to the extreme outer edge of the fabric while you are not stitching. This avoids marking the fabric.

MATERIALS

You will need an evenweave fabric which is a fabric which has the same number of weft (horizontal) threads as it has warp (vertical) threads.

LINEN

This is a natural fibre so the thickness of the threads may vary across the fabric. Linen is also more expensive than Aida but as you stitch over two threads (Fig.1), it is much easier to use when you are stitching quarter, three-quarter and special shaping stitches.

Fig. 1. A full cross stitch worked over two threads on linen.

AIDA

Beginners may find it easier to stitch on Aida. The threads are woven in blocks which makes them easier to count and your stitches will look more even. You generally stitch over one block (Fig. 2).

Fig. 2. A full cross stitch worked over one block on Aida fabric.

WASTE CANVAS

This versatile material enables you to stitch a design onto almost anything – pillowslips, T-shirts, jumpers. Baste the waste canvas onto your chosen item and then stitch your design as normal. When you've finished, unpick the basting stitches. Gently dampen your work and pull out the waste canvas with tweezers. If you pull out the vertical threads first, the horizontal threads will then be easier to remove.

DESIGN SIZE

It is important to know the 'count' of fabric you choose, as this will determine the finished size of your design. The finer the fabric, the smaller the stitches e.g. '18-count' Aida means there are 18 blocks to the inch, therefore producing 18 stitches to the inch. If you use '14-count' Aida your finished design will be larger as you are stitching with 14 squares to the inch. When you work on linen you stitch over two threads, so if you stitch on 32 count linen you will have 16 stitches to the inch.

Always remember to allow about 2½ in (6.5 cm) on each side of the design for stretching and framing.

THREADS

I have used DMC threads in my designs as the choice of colours is superb and the quality is beautiful. There are also other brands available that you can use.

STRANDED COTTON (FLOSS)

This is made up of six strands of mercerised cotton that can be separated into single strands or groups of two or more. Most of the designs in this book are worked with two strands for cross stitches and one strand for backstitching. If you prefer a softer image, use one strand for cross stitches. Always pull one strand out at a time then put the two strands together.

PERLE COTTON

This is a mercerised thread that is non-divisible and has a soft gloss when stitched.

FLOWER THREAD

This is a non-divisible matt yarn designed mainly for work on fine fabrics eg linen.

BE ORGANISED

A thread organiser is invaluable. It is a piece of card with holes punched down each side. You can easily make one yourself.

Once you have chosen the colours you need, cut them into half-metre lengths or 1 metre lengths and thread them through the holes (Fig. 3). Label them with the colour number and when you need to use one length of thread you just remove the thread from the organiser, take off the required number of strands and replace the rest back in the thread organiser.

Fig. 3. A thread organiser.

FRAMES

It is personal preference whether or not you use a frame or embroidery hoop. It depends a lot on your stitching tension but as a rule, using an embroidery hoop makes stitching easier. It keeps your fabric taut and does not let it stretch.

NEEDLES

For all counted needlework you will need a blunt tapestry needle. I use a size 24 tapestry needle as it is very comfortable to hold without being too thin or too chunky. For working on waste canvas you will need a crewel needle, which has a sharp point and flat eye enabling several strands to be used at once, or as required.

CHARTS

Each colour on the chart represents a colour of thread. Each square of colour represents one cross stitch. The backstitching is identified by solid lines. You will probably find it easier working in blocks of colour than rows. You will also find it helpful to have a few needles threaded with different colours, so when you change to a different colour you are ready to stitch.

LET'S BEGIN!

The first thing to do is find the centre of the fabric. To do this fold your fabric in half both ways. The centre is the best place to begin stitching, as your work will then be correctly positioned on the fabric. You can put long tacking stitches across and down to mark the centre. Remove these when you have started your work.

All your underneath stitches must run in the same direction, so that all your top stitches will also be going the same way. Don't stitch one cross at a time unless it is a single cross stitch in a different colour to the surrounding stitches. Stitch in a row — if you have 10 cross stitches to work, stitch the 10 underneath stitches first then turn back on yourself and complete the crosses.

STARTING AND FINISHING WITHOUT USING A KNOT

STARTING

Try not to use knots, as these look very unsightly when the design is finished and stretched. Anchor your thread in place by bringing your needle up through the back of the fabric where you are ready to start. Leave a tail long enough to be caught by your next few stitches and then trim the end. Look at the back of your work to check that the tail has been secured.

FINISHING OFF

To finish off without using a knot weave the thread through the backs of four or five adjacent stitches and trim the end.

CROSS STITCHES EXPLAINED

FULL CROSS STITCHES ON AIDA

To make one cross stitch, think of the stitch area as a square of four holes. Bring the needle up through the hole in the bottom left corner of the square and then down through the hole in the top right corner. Then take the needle up through the bottom right hole and down into the top left hole.

To stitch a row of cross stitches in the same colour bring your needle up at the bottom left hole and down in the top right hole. Do not finish the stitch but continue this step until you complete the correct number of stitches going one way. Then work back along the row to complete your cross stitches i.e. from bottom right to top left.

FULL CROSS STITCHES ON LINEN

To stitch a single cross stitch on linen, do as above but stitch across two threads.

QUARTER STITCHES

These are indicated by a colour in a corner of a square. Work a quarter stitch as shown in Fig. 4. If you are using Aida, you will have to split the centre threads on the Aida with your needle. You will often find two quarter stitches in the same block but using different colours. This is stitched very simply by stitching your first quarter stitch in one colour then when you work your second quarter stitch in the second colour, push your needle into the same hole in the centre of the block. Backstitches over the top after you have finished all your cross stitching will hide any spaces.

Fig. 4. Quarter stitch.

HALF-CROSS STITCHES
This is half of a full cross stitch – in other words a diagonal stitch. It is usually used as shading in the designs in this book.

THREE-QUARTER STITCHES
I have used these stitches primarily with the special shaping stitches (described below). Work a quarter stitch as described above and then make a diagonal half stitch across it (Fig. 5).

Fig. 5. Three-quarter stitch.

SPECIAL SHAPING STITCHES
I created this stitch to give gentle sloping lines in and around the edge of the designs.

It is stitched over two blocks. This is indicated on the charts by three-quarters of a square being in a colour and a quarter of the next square being in the same colour. Therefore you stitch a three-quarter stitch and a quarter stitch (Fig. 6). Your backstitching over the top will complete the design, shown below by a dotted line.

Fig. 6. Special shaping stitch.

BACKSTITCHING
Backstitching is shown by a continuous line and should be worked after the design has been completed. When the chart shows a backstitch across a cross stitch, the backstitch should be worked on the top of the stitch.

FRENCH KNOTS
This will be indicated on the chart by a dot. To stitch, bring the needle up where you want the knot to be. Hold the thread as it comes out of the fabric and place the needle behind it. Twist the needle twice around the thread and insert the needle back into the fabric slightly away from where you started, keeping the thread taut all the time (Fig. 7). Practice this on a spare piece of fabric.

Fig. 7. French knot.

Lazy Daisy Stitches

Bring the needle up at 1 and down at 2 (which is very slightly away from 1), without pulling the thread all the way through the fabric and so leaving a loop. Bring it up at 3, inside the loop and pull gently to secure the loop, then push the needle into the fabric at 4 (Fig. 8). Repeat where shown on the chart.

Fig. 8. Lazy daisy stitch.

Long Stitches

Long stitches are quite literally long stitches – where they are shown on the charts, just stitch that whole length with one stitch.

FINISHING AND FRAMING

Looking After Your Fabric

It is inevitable that your work will require washing after being completed. The threads are meant to be colourfast, but to be on the safe side, take great care when washing. Immerse your work in lukewarm soapy water and gently wash by hand. Do not rub vigorously. Dry flat face down on a towel and iron on the reverse side to prevent the stitches being flattened.

Lacing

Cut a piece of acid-free mount board to the same size as the inside of your frame. Centre your work on the board and insert pins along the top edge. Use the fabric holes to help you keep the edges straight. Gently pull the fabric and pin along the bottom edge in the same way. Repeat with the sides. Turn your project over and with a large-eyed needle and crochet cotton (which must be knotted) lace the fabric from top to bottom using an under-and-over movement. Then repeat from side to side (Fig. 9). Stitch the corners down and remove the pins – you can now frame your work.

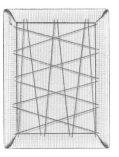

Fig. 9. Lacing.

Framing

Mounting into Gift Cards

The cards used in this book have been mounted in 3-fold cards. A wide variety of cards are available in needlework or craft shops. Follow the manufacturer's instructions for mounting your work.

Mounting onto Flexi-hoops

Centre your design in the flexi-hoop and place in the flexi-hoop. Trim the spare fabric on the back to 1 in (2.5 cm). I usually put some wadding in the middle to give some density to the picture. Lace the ends across the back of the flexi-hoop and then glue a piece of felt over them.

Suppliers

For the name of your local stockist of DMC threads and Zweigart Aida, contact:

DMC Creative World Ltd:
Pullman Road
Wigston, Leicestershire
LE18 2DY
United Kingdom
0116 281 1040

Dollfus-Mieg & Cia
Arts Du Fil
13, Rue de Pfastatt
F-68057 Mulhouse Cedex
France
33 1 49281000

Zweigart & Sawitzki
Fronäcker Str. 50
71063 Sindelfingen
Germany
49 7031 795 5

Handar
Emdenstraat 9
NL-7418 BR
Deventer Holland
31 570 623 586

Dollfus-Mieg & Cia S.A.
Caspe, 30
E-08010 Barcelona
Spain
34 3 3177436

Dollfus-Mieg & Cia S.P.A.
Viale Italia 84
1-20020 Lainate (Milano)
Italy
39 2 93570427
or
Stafil GmbH
Altmannstr. 1
1-39100 Bozen
Italy
39 471 916007

Joan Toggitt Ltd
Weston Canal Plaza
2 Riverview Drive
Somerset, New Jersey
08873 USA
1 732 2711949

Acknowledgements

There are so many people I would like to thank for helping and supporting me with this, my first book.
My wonderful husband Graham, my mum and my children, Danielle, David and Richard, for all their encouragement and support.
Helena Mottershead whose help with the designs made this book possible. Pauline Wright for printing and checking all the thread counts and keeping me supplied with endless cups of coffee. Helen Chambers for all the charting and colouring of the charts. Joanne Hemsley for proofreading my book.
All of my staff at Designer Stitches for every bit of help they gave me. All my stitchers for pulling out all the stops: Danielle (my daughter), Jackie Hrycan, Julie Cartwright, Gill Schnieden, Nicola Northrop, Sue Deacon, Sue Cottrell, Lynn Robinson, Mary Mills, Kay Cartwright and Elaine Sharp. And Pat Marsh for believing in me.
Sara Kidd for her design, Shona Wood for her photography and all those who helped at Collins & Brown.

I would also like to thank the following companies for the supplies used in this book:
DMC for all their threads.
IL-Soft for their superb computer design programme.
Heebee Designs Ltd, Knutsford for their supplies of fabric.
Terry at the Frame Workshop in Altrincham, Cheshire for all the stretching and lacing of the finished designs.
Framecraft Miniatures, Birmingham for their trinket boxes.